UP

WORKING
AT 50+

WORKING AT 50+

MALCOLM HORNBY

LIFEGUIDES

AUTHOR

Malcolm Hornby, Chartered FCIPD, MCMI, is a writer and business and personal coach. He has worked for the Civil Service, taught chemistry, physics and biology, worked in sales and sales management and also in management training and HR. He also spent three years teaching Human Resources on the Open University's MBA programme and is the author of *Get that Job* (Prentice-Hall). His website is www.hornby.org

LifeGuides are commissioned and published by Help the Aged, 207–221 Pentonville Road, London N1 9UZ and can be purchased via www.helptheaged.org.uk or from bookshops

For a full list of Help the Aged publications, see the website, telephone 020 7239 1946 or email publications@helptheaged.org.uk.

First published 2008

Trade distribution by Turnaround Publisher Services Ltd

British Library Cataloguing in Publication Data
A catalogue record for this book is available from the British Library

ISBN 978-1-84598-026-9

Designed and typeset by Price Watkins Design
Printed and bound in England by CPI Mackay Ltd

CONTENTS

CONTENTS, continued

INTRODUCTION

G ood health care, improved diet and a better quality of life have paid dividends for all of us. Our life expectancy continues to increase rapidly. In 1945 the average life expectancy for men was 63. Now it is 77. On average, women lived to the age of 68 in 1945 whereas now they live to 81.

Today, some 20 million people in the UK are aged over 50 – a third of the population. That percentage is set to grow. In the decade since 1997 the number of workers aged 50–69 has increased by 1.6 million – an increase of about 27 per cent.

When the Old Age Pension was introduced, in 1908, it guaranteed an income for everyone over 70. But then there were ten workers for every pensioner. At present there are four workers for every pensioner and economists predict that by 2050 there will be just two workers for every retired person.

The raising of the state retirement age and the collapse of so many company pension schemes are just two reasons why people need to continue working and earning through their middle years. People of 50+, with their accumulated skills, knowledge and experience, are a huge national asset. Yet, sadly, they often find it difficult to get work.

LIVE LONG ...AND PROSPER

Many people simply cannot wait to retire early: this book is not for them. It aims to help people of 50 and over get back into employment and stay in employment for as long as they choose to work.

The working environment and employment opportunities have never been better for older workers. The UK is facing a skills shortage. The pool of twenty- and thirtysomethings continues to diminish while the number of fiftysomethings and above is growing ever bigger. They represent a valuable national resource – a huge supply of experienced, mature and skilled workers. Many employers have recognised this and many are now seeking to adopt an 'age-positive' philosophy and build an age-diverse workforce.

Add to this new mindset the fact that the law has strengthened in favour of older workers. The Employment Equality (Age) Regulations (2006) mean that if you apply for a job and are turned down because of your age, the employer is breaking the law.

Despite all this, older candidates often miss out. In the course of the research for this book, three recurring themes emerged which appear to suggest why.

BARRIERS TO GETTING A JOB

The three key reasons why older job seekers can find it more difficult to find work seem to be:

- low self-esteem; writing yourself off; undervaluing your skills and experience

- an aversion to/avoidance of information technology. In today's workplace up-to-date computer skills – at the very least, word-processing, email and using the internet – are essential. The internet is a crucial job-search tool, and many employers simply do not accept applications by traditional mail any longer. In addition, many jobs require basic computer skills

- many employers claim that applications from people aged 50+ are no different from applications from any other candidates – but over-50s need to use all the skills any other applicant would. They need to produce a strong application which matches the candidate to the job and to perform well at interview.

This book therefore has three major objectives:

- to help you to recognise and value yourself in the job marketplace and to raise your self-esteem

- to help you to become more familiar with information technology, which will give you access to the phenomenal number of job opportunities available through the internet

- to bring your job-hunting skills up to date so that you can seek, find and win the job that you want.

As for age discrimination, it may still be the most common form of workplace discrimination in the UK, but by being aware of the potential barriers and knowing how to approach them, you can put yourself in a strong position to overcome them.

THE FUTURE

As the over-50s become an ever more significant proportion of the population, society will increasingly depend on the contribution they can make. By 2020 the UK will have 3 million more people of 50+ and a million fewer under-50s than it has today in 2008. That means fewer people to support the older generation. So older workers *will* come into their own.

Indeed, they are already doing so. Of today's 50+ generation (up to age 60 for women, 65 for men) 72 per cent are working (as compared with 81 per cent of 25–49-year-olds), and over the last few years the 50+ group has shown the fastest growth rate in employment. The culture of early retirement, prevalent in the 1980s and 1990s, has evaporated. The Government has said that it wants another 1 million older workers in the workforce.

Getting older as a nation is something which we should celebrate. For many of us, living longer will mean spending more years in retirement. By working and earning longer, we can ensure that those retirement years are enjoyable and fulfilling. ■

1

THE FIRST DAY OF THE REST OF YOUR LIFE

THE FIRST DAY OF THE REST OF YOUR LIFE

'I have always believed that each man makes his own happiness and is responsible for his own problems.' *(Ray Kroc)*

What do you want to do when you grow up? Perhaps you are reading this book because you have come to a point in your life where you have made a decision to change job? Or perhaps someone else has made that decision for you? Maybe you are ready for a complete change of direction and a complete life-makeover, including a new job. Or maybe you have been working as – say – a store manager for years, you are a good store manager, your circumstances have changed and you want to get another job as a store manager. Whichever is the case, this book can help you achieve your goal.

CAREER AND LIFE PLANNING

You are probably reading this book because you want to make a significant change in your life, so to start with stand back and think about the career decisions you have taken over the years. What did you want to do when you were a youngster? How have things developed and evolved? And finally – and more importantly – where to from here?

YOU'RE NEVER TOO OLD ...

If you are sitting reading this thinking 'Well, I'm over 50. I'm way too old for major career change. Who's going to employ someone of my age?', or 'I wouldn't know where to begin thinking about creating my own job', or indeed any other negative thoughts about your continued success, then how's this for a reality check?

Ray Kroc was of Czechoslovakian descent and worked as an ambulance driver in the First World War. He subsequently moved to the USA and tried his hand at a number of jobs. By the early 1950s, he was a Multimixer milkshake machine salesman. Two of his customers were the McDonald brothers Dick and Mac, who were using eight of his machines at their innovative California hamburger restaurant. The brothers had recognised the potential of their business and had started to franchise it, but with minimal success. Kroc believed that the restaurant model had tremendous potential, and in 1955, at the age of 52, he acquired franchising rights to open a McDonald's restaurant of his own, in Des Plaines, Illinois.

> 'I was 52 years old. I had diabetes and incipient arthritis. I had lost my gall bladder and most of my thyroid gland in earlier campaigns, but I was convinced that the best was ahead of me.' *(Ray Kroc)*

It was the McDonald brothers who invented the Speedee Service System, which established the principles of modern fast-food restaurants, but it was Ray Kroc who recognised the enormous potential. He encouraged the brothers to put him in charge of franchising, and founded the McDonald's Corporation with the opening of his first franchise.

Within six years Ray Kroc went from travelling salesman to successful businessman, and in 1961 he bought out the McDonald brothers for US$2.7 million. It is Ray Kroc who is credited in the history books as being the founder of the international brand McDonald's.

Ray Kroc died in 1984 at the age of 81 having built up a fortune of $500 million in less than 30 years. He once said: 'If you work just for money, you'll never make it, but if you love what you're doing and you always put the customer first, success will be yours.'

Ray Kroc's success is a lesson to all of us that life can begin at 50 if you have the passion and enthusiasm for what you want to achieve.

Although most people of 50+ will not be expecting to launch a multi-million-dollar enterprise, and may well have to accept that their highest-earning days are behind them, there is a great deal that can be done to improve the chances of finding suitable work and achieving a healthy income for the future.

MOTIVATION MANAGEMENT

Really knowing what you want out of the next stage of your life has to be the basis of your approach to your job hunt.

When you started off in your career you probably had a few things to prove – maybe to your family, your peers or yourself. Motivation to earn a good income and to achieve something you could be proud of were probably quite high and these factors may still be high on your agenda. But maybe things have changed.

Why, at the age of 50+, do you want to work? On the face of it this is an easy question to answer, but maybe not quite that easy when you really begin to think. (Statistics show that the reason most often cited for early retirement is ill health – ahead of redundancy – but 50 per cent of those who retire because of ill health say they are keen to work again.)

Make some time for yourself and think about what you want to get out of the rest of your life, so that you can look for a job in the context of your life goals.

What motivates us often changes as we grow older. As children, our greatest needs may be winning the love of our parents. As we grow and mature new values, such as autonomy, achievement and the need for self-approval, become important. Becoming a parent or a grandparent may shift the emphasis yet again.

It can be easy to lose touch with what matters most to us in the process of managing our day-to-day lives, and because few of us stop to reflect on our values we fail to challenge the way we see the world.

Understanding your personal motivators can help you:

- plan personal and career goals
- decide on the way you behave at work
- understand the kind of people you most like to associate with

■ allocate your finances and time to achieve the greatest personal satisfaction.

Different things motivate different individuals. Some people appear to be motivated almost exclusively by money while others are motivated by the prestige of being part of a special group or team. Still others are motivated by recognition and rewards other than money.

In the late 1960s Abraham Maslow developed a hierarchical theory of human needs. Presented in pyramid form (see page 19), it shows our basic needs at the bottom of the pyramid while our less tangible ambitions are associated with those needs near the top of the pyramid: self-actualisation.

Maslow suggested a hierarchy of five levels of basic needs. He suggested that needs at lower levels needed to be satisfied (at least partially) before we can move on to higher levels. He also suggested that an over-supply of 'lower-order' needs does not necessarily increase motivation. Let's say you meet someone who is hungry and you offer to feed them in return for that person washing your car. Once they have had their fill of food, they will not be able eat any more and no matter how much food you pile in front of them you probably will not be able to motivate them to wash more cars, because you have satisfied their lower-order need. An offer of regular car-washing duties might motivate them to more work, but this could be satisfying the needs of safety and belonging. This is a very simplified view of Maslow's theory.

To a large extent money is a 'lower-order needs' satisfier – you can't buy happiness, but you can satisfy many of your lower-order needs with it, whereas, at the top of the pyramid, no amount of money will make you a talented concert pianist, a composer or a revered artist.

That said, we cannot ignore the fact that money is probably the biggest motivator for continuing working. Many of us have seen our pension funds diminish and the returns we expected simply will not be there. Paul Lewis, the writer and broadcaster who presents BBC Radio 4's *Moneybox*, says: 'A penny saved in mid-life is worth tuppence in later life.' While you are fit and healthy it makes sense to work and build up reserves for unforeseeable future expense such as repairs to the home, and choices we make like helping our children to buy their first home. Money saved in mid-life will also mean that we will have less to worry about as we reach old age and can have a more fulfilling life than might have been possible had we not continued working.

Absence of motivators can cause you to move back to lower levels. If someone is having problems with their marriage (level 3) they are unlikely to be motivated to achieve their sales target (level 4). If someone is having their house re-possessed (level 2) they are unlikely to be focusing on working as a team member (level 3).

MASLOW'S MOTIVATION THEORY

Level 5
SELF-ACTUALISATION
Self-fulfilment, growth,
accomplishment

Level 4
SELF-ESTEEM
Self-respect, status, recognition,
independence, dignity, freedom

Level 3
SOCIAL NEEDS
Family, belonging to group(s), social activities,
love, friendship, marriage, avoiding loneliness

Level 2
SAFETY NEEDS
Security, protection from danger, routine,
order, freedom from anxiety

Level 1
PHYSIOLOGICAL NEEDS
Hunger, thirst, sleep, clothing, warmth, sex

So what are your motivators for getting that new job? What's driving you? Has your pension fund underperformed, or has some unanticipated life event dictated that you will have to carry on earning a living? At the other end of the pyramid, perhaps you are in a position of financial independence and your greatest motivator is to do something where at last you will be recognised for your outstanding knowledge and experience. Or maybe, perhaps like someone who works for a charity, your work needs are in the middle and you need to belong to a team.

What do you want to get out of a new job? Sit down with a notepad and write a list of the things you want. Here are a few to trigger your thoughts, but add as many things as you can think of that you would like to get from your ideal job:

- advancement opportunities
- flexible hours
- fully utilising skills/talents
- getting credit for a job well done
- go-ahead employer
- good basic pay
- having a say
- interest/enjoyment
- job security
- learning new skills
- physical working conditions
- sense of accomplishment
- skilled management
- sufficient help/equipment
- working for a boss you respect.

Work is only a part of your life and it may well be that needs at different levels are satisfied in your home life; maybe only a small need has to be filled to complete the picture, and this can be done by working. Of course, your need to work might have nothing to do with

Maslow's criteria – it may well be that if you and your partner inhabit the same space 24/7 it will drive the pair of you crazy. But we are all different, and really thinking about exactly what you want out of your next job will help you enormously in your job search.

A BETTER WORK/LIFE BALANCE FOR THE FUTURE: SEVEN IDEAS TO CHANGE YOUR LIFE

Statistics show that people in the UK spend more time at work than their counterparts elsewhere in Europe, yet there is no evidence that they are more successful or happier than the Continental workers. How can we manage our lives better and get the balance between work and play right? How can you develop and achieve the career and life that you want? The answer could lie in establishing your priorities in life and developing a career and life plan – and then turning your ideas into reality.

The seven ideas on pages 23–9 will help you develop a greater awareness of what you need and want out of life, so that your career fits into the life you want, rather than fitting your life into your career. We will then look at how you can turn your dreams into reality using a coach as a sounding-board for your ideas.

DO YOU HAVE A LIFE PLAN?

Most people appear to spend more time choosing a new car than they would ever spend planning what they want to do with the rest of their lives. When asked the question 'Do you have a life plan?' the vast majority of people will say 'no'.

But if the question is 'Do you work for an organisation that has a strategic plan?' most employed people will say they do. So the irony is that although we want to work for organisations that have a sense of purpose and direction, few of us apply the same principles to our own lives.

The responsibility for managing your career, and your life, is yours.

It is not the responsibility of your parents, your partner, your previous teachers, your boss or your organisation, or anyone else for that matter. Yet many people are stressed-out, doing jobs they hate, working every waking hour to try to meet the expectations of others.

Job seekers often follow a similar pattern, looking for a clone of their previous job, even though they did not really enjoy it – because they (wrongly) believe it is all they know how to do.

Like Ray Kroc, we are in charge of our own destiny, and those of us who have the advantage of living in a Western society can, to a very large extent, shape our own future.

If you embrace and act on the following ideas they will help you develop a greater awareness of what you need and want out of life, so that your career fits into the life you want, rather than the other way round.

WE ARE ALL MORTAL ('*CARPE DIEM*')

None of us is immortal. There will come a time when each of us will make our exit. Some people believe that their time on earth is predetermined and that their lives are 'fated' – 'what will be will be'. However, to a very large extent we can be masters of our own destiny.

Instead of accepting whatever life throws at us, we should 'seize the day' (*carpe diem*). Once a day has passed, you will never have the opportunity to live it again. If you want a wake-up call for how many days you have left, try this little exercise. Draw a horizontal line on a piece of paper. At the left end of the line write a zero and also the year you were born. Then try to guess how old you will be when you die (see page 9 for the average ages) and write this number and the year at the right end of the line. Now draw a cross on the line to

correspond with your age now. How do you feel about the time that has passed? How do you feel about the days and years to come?

If you believe that you are in control of your life, and you want to make the most of it, read on.

Idea 1: define your vision of success

Are you successful? Do you want to be successful? What is success? And how do we recognise success?

- She must be successful – she drives a Porsche.
- He really must have made it – all of his suits are Hugo Boss.
- They must be successful – they live in a big, detached house and take three holidays a year.

Are any of these *your* idea of success?

While it is certainly not wrong to be inspired by people whom we admire, we should not try to copy their lives, or live a life that is dictated by the desires of others. A dictionary definition of success is 'the favourable outcome of something which one has attempted'. What does success mean to you? What was your knee-jerk reaction to that question? A big salary increase? A promotion? A fast car? When did you last sit down and write your definition of 'a successful life' – if you have ever done so at all? There are as many definitions as there are people reading this book. And the definition does not have to be driven by money. After all, many people would assert that they achieved the greatest success of their life working as a volunteer, helping people who really needed what they had to offer, even though the financial reward was nil.

So what are *your* criteria for a successful life? What is *your* life vision? Remember, a vision is a dream taken seriously. Write down the words that come into your head and develop *your* definition of success.

Idea 2: write a life plan – develop your strategy

Where do you want to get to in your life? What do you want to achieve? What is *your* life plan?

In other words, 'What do you want to do with the rest of your life?'

Most people are too busy with the day-to-day issues of their lives to establish a strategic direction and to set life goals. But just as organisations usually have a long-term strategy, there is much to be gained by applying the same principles to ourselves. As a starting point, write down 5–10 'life goals' for the next five-year period. These are the actions which can turn your vision into reality.

Idea 3: develop a positive attitude

People often have problems in making career plans and developing goals because they impose barriers on themselves. They say, or think, things like 'I could never achieve this', 'That opportunity is not available to me', 'I'm too old to ...', etc. This seems to become an increasing problem with older career changers and job hunters.

How many times have you heard the question 'Is the glass half-full or half-empty?' and felt good about the positive 'half-full' answer that you've given? If you think about it, though, this is not really all that positive, because unless you live your life in a vacuum, the glass is *always* full: sometimes with water, sometimes air, sometimes both, sometimes poison, sometimes nectar. The 'glass' is in your hands. The responsibility for making the most of the contents is, to a very large extent, yours. If you adopt the mindset that you can make the most of what you have, you are half-way to success.

'Too many candidates de-select themselves, often through lack of confidence. My mother-in-law (60) went for an interview at a media company last year. She withdrew from the interview process after the first interview because she didn't feel that it was right for a group of lovely, lively young people to be "lumbered with an old fogey like me" (incidentally, she is *not* an old fogey). She was making assumptions about their preferences.' *(professional recruiter)*

Many successful sports people develop mental pictures of themselves crossing the winning line first, or scoring that winning goal. You can do something similar.

Convince yourself that you are in charge of your own destiny. Believe that you can achieve the success you want, picture yourself achieving it, and you are on your way to doing so.

Idea 4: prepare to change

Computer technology and the internet have given us a new way of doing business. You probably have more computing power in your mobile phone than existed in the entire world at the start of the 1960s. Technology has changed the way we work forever. There are now about 25 per cent fewer secretaries employed than there were ten years ago. Change often means the end of certain types of job and the creation of new ones. Indeed, many organisations now value themselves in terms of their 'human capital' (their work force). Career and life planning is about helping you to capitalise on your own human assets and take advantage of present and future job opportunities. We live in a world of constant flux and as many traditional jobs are disappearing new ones are emerging.

Career and life planning is a personal change-management process. We have all heard it said that 'people don't like change'. It is by no means always true. If people do not like change, why do we look forward to going on holiday, buying new clothes, getting a new car ...? People like change if it answers the 'What's in it for me?' question in a positive way.

Flexibility and adaptability are the qualities we need to cope with change.

Charles Darwin tells us that 'the most successful species are the ones which adapt best to the changing environment. The most successful individuals are the ones with the greatest competitive advantage over the others.' He could have been writing a career guide for the 21st century. So how do you make the most of change? By keeping an open mind, having a positive attitude to change, and identifying what's in it for you.

'We have a flexible approach to employing staff and [adopt a] "best person for the job" philosophy regardless of age, so the over-50s, even over-60s can easily be employed if they have the right attitude. Some roles can be flexible in terms of hours worked. The biggest gap at this stage is IT skills: in this day and age these are very important.' *(Glynis Frew, Director, Hunters Property Group Ltd)*

'I find most older jobseekers have accepted that they need to accept change, and to keep up with modern working practices. A lot of them have taken IT courses, for instance.' *(John Davis, Regional Employer Engagement Team, Jobcentre Plus)*

Idea 5: re-invent yourself

You may need to challenge your self-image and what you can achieve. In business, 'paradigm paralysis' can cause missed opportunities. Swiss watch manufacturers dismissed the concept of the quartz watch, even though they had invented the technology, and suffered the consequences. No fewer than 42 companies rejected Chester Carlson's new photographic process in 1930. One company – the Xerox Corporation – saw the opportunity, and produced the first photocopier.

Inertia or fear sometimes stops people from challenging their personal paradigm – their idea of what they think they are. You have not been genetically encoded to be a secretary, an accountant, a trainer … you can take control and have the life that you want, but you need to be brave: 'You cannot discover new lands until you have the courage to lose sight of the shore' (André Gide).

Paradigm shifts can create new opportunities. One example of a successful paradigm shift is Lucozade. In the mid-20th century Lucozade was a drink for helping people to recover after a period of illness. In the 1980s Lucozade re-invented itself completely and extremely successfully as an 'energy' drink for athletes and sports people.

What has Lucozade got to do with career and life planning? Everything. Our working environments are changing faster than ever. The rate of change continues to accelerate. A couple of decades ago, no one had heard of HTML, SQL, C++ or Java. Now people who can 'speak' these IT and website assembly languages can virtually dictate their salary. There is no single way to plan your career or to find a new job: the keys to maximising your potential are flexibility, keeping an open mind and regarding change as an opportunity, not a threat.

Our beliefs and perceptions about what is right or possible often prevent us from exploring new solutions. You have only one life. Challenge your life paradigm. Just like Lucozade, you may need to re-invent yourself to achieve your goals.

Sometimes, perhaps following redundancy or the closure of the company they were working for, people of 50+ who have until that point in their careers held high-level, high-earning positions find themselves job-hunting — and competing with much less experienced but somewhat younger candidates. The people interviewing may be younger and less experienced themselves than the 50+ candidates, and may feel threatened by their experience; another factor could be the previous salary, which may suggest that the 50+ candidate could not possibly be interested in any position carrying a lower one. Hence, through no fault of their own, the older candidate is already at a disadvantage.

In such situations, it helps to realise that you are at a career crossroads, and you may have to adjust your expectations — or indeed, consider becoming self-employed (see chapter 6).

A former marketing director in his 60s who had worked in the construction industry found it impossible to get any sort of a job at a similar level. He came to the conclusion that the industry he had been part of was 'a young man's game' and settled, initially reluctantly, for a job as an insurance adviser. 'Originally I would have liked a similar role at a similar level,' he commented a while later, 'but looking back I realise that the job I have got is just fine, with little responsibility, surrounded by young people — and it's a job where I can use my life skills.'

Idea 6: prepare to fail

Embarking on a job-search programme can be challenging, enjoyable and rewarding. Job searching can also be very depressing, because job searches for sales managers, marketing directors, nurses, fitters, account-ants, product managers and so on all look like this:

no	no	no	no	no	no	no	no	no	no
no	no	no	no	no	no	no	no	no	no
no	no	no	no	no	no	no	no	no	no
no	no	no	no	no	no	no	no	no	no
no	no	no	no	no	no	no	no	no	no
no	no	no	no	no	no	no	no	no	**YES!**

Sometimes there are more nos, sometimes not so many. Since few of us are good at taking 'no', it is hardly surprising that many peo-ple, having begun their job search with a burst of enthusiasm, become anxious, then filled with self-doubt, then depressed. The effect is com-pounded if you are out of work.

However, you *can* succeed in spite of initial failure, as long as you are persistent and persevere. If you do not believe that you can still succeed after failure, take note of some 'failures' that were never going to make it: Coca-Cola, Ford, Gillette and Heinz. You may recall that they all went on to better things, but:

- Coca-Cola sold only 400 bottles in its first year in business
- Henry Ford went bust twice before his business took off
- in its first year of trading Gillette sold only 51 safety razors and 168 blades
- H. J. Heinz (of beanz fame) went bankrupt, learned the lessons, and did better next time.

Here are some others: Luciano Pavarotti was told that he should follow in his family's footsteps and remain a baker as he would never succeed as a singer. John Lennon's Auntie Mimi used to tell him daily that he would never get rich strumming that guitar. Eric Morecambe's mum received a letter from his teacher saying 'I hate to say this, but your Eric will never get anywhere in life'. (A recent BBC poll voted Eric Morecambe the Funniest Man of the Century.) Darius and The Cheeky Girls achieved chart success despite rejections at the start. Paul McCartney was not considered a good enough singer to join the school choir. Clint Eastwood was fired by Universal Studios because of his broken tooth, protuberant Adam's apple and slow speech delivery. And the manager of the Grand Ole Opry fired a young singer called Elvis Presley, telling him, 'You ain't goin' nowhere, son. You ought to go back to drivin' a truck'.

What a different world it would be if these people had heeded the advice they received.

Many famous authors – Graham Greene is just one example – had their books rejected by publishers. In recent times, some authors have self-published and subsequently been signed up by a publisher. The message is: don't be afraid of failure – treat it as a learning opportunity. You may have to kiss a lot of frogs before you find your prince, but if you persevere you *can* succeed.

Idea 7: do it now! *Carpe diem*

When you embark on a career and life planning process, do not rush it. You might find it takes several hours over the space of a week or two. Follow the principles below. It may feel like hard work, but the investment will pay off.

CAREER AND LIFE PLANNING TECHNIQUES

These career and life planning techniques will help you to establish your real priorities in life, so that you can use them as the foundation of your career plan and job hunt.

■ **Mind-map** Use a mind-map to help you to define your

vision of success. Write the word 'success' in the middle of a bubble in the centre of a large piece of paper. Now let your mind free-wheel with all the ideas that can make it a reality. You will find a sample mind-map on page 146. For further information on mind-mapping, see chapter 7, which lists further sources of help.

- **Work/life balance and life pies** Analyse your life over a period of time – say, a week. Log how much time you spend doing various things: working, travelling to work, socialising, spending time with your family, etc. Use a pie chart to represent this. Then draw your 'ideal' life pie. Your headings might include: community and professional activities, continuing education, entertainment, financial management, fun, hobbies, household maintenance, housekeeping, personal development, professional development, reading, relationships, shopping, spending time with friends, sports, surfing the net, travelling to work, watching TV, attending a place of worship, work. Visit www.eoslifework.co.uk/getalife.xls for a Microsoft Excel tool to help you to do this.

- **Force-field analysis on your life** This comprises a list of positives and negatives. On the right side of a piece of paper list everything negative that is holding you back in your current situation. On the left side list all the positives that can take your life forward.

- **SWOT analysis** Analyse your strengths, weaknesses, opportunities and threats. You may have come across SWOT analysis at work or used it to analyse business situations. SWOT stands for strengths, weaknesses, opportunities and threats. Using a SWOT analysis on yourself can be an extremely useful technique for helping you to think about what you can offer in the job market. Divide a piece of paper into four quarters. In the top left area write 'Strengths'; then put 'Weaknesses' at top right,

'Opportunities' bottom left, and finally 'Threats' bottom right. Now fill it in. The SWOT analysis will help you to take stock of your position so that you can plan what you want to do next. The strengths and weaknesses elements are personal to you. Opportunities and threats lie in the external environment.

- **Goal-setting** List all the things you would like to achieve in your life, and then prioritise them.
- **Personality profiling/self-analysis** Take online tests to gain greater personal insight. The website www.keirsey.com is a good starting point – see also pages 89–106.
- **Obituary** Write your own obituary for today, then write it for ten years from now. How do the two differ? It sounds morbid, but writing your obituary can help you to think clearly about your past and future life. If you feel uncomfortable at the thought of this exercise, try this alternative: imagine that you have suddenly become famous and tomorrow you will be interviewed by a chat-show host such as Michael Parkinson or Sir David Frost; write some notes on what you will tell them about yourself. Now do the same for an interview taking place ten years from now.

Using these techniques to start a journey of career and life planning is only the start, of course. If you want to achieve a better work/life balance, you need to commit time and energy to the process. If you have a partner, you must involve him or her from the start, so that you can develop a joint vision and set mutually compatible life goals.

If the above has inspired you to do something, set yourself a time to do it. Switch off the TV tonight and start on your career and life plan. You only have one life, so do not be like the person who bought a motivational audio course on procrastination but never got round to listening to it.

And remember, a successful life is a journey, not a destination: make sure that you review and re-set your goals periodically.

If you tell yourself that you cannot achieve your vision of a successful life, you will not achieve it. Tell yourself that you can achieve your vision of a successful life and you might achieve it (and you probably will). To sum up: *if you try, you might; if you don't, you won't.*

IMPROVE YOUR CHANCES OF SUCCESS: GET A COACH

'There is no such thing as a "self-made" man. We are made up of thousands of others. Everyone who has ever done a kind deed for us, or spoken one word of encouragement to us, has entered into the make-up of our character and of our thoughts, as well as our success.' *(George Matthew Adams)*

A coach will help you to turn your visions and dreams of your career/life plan into reality. Do you know someone whom you can use as a sounding-board for your ideas? As you develop your career/life plan, you will find it very beneficial to bounce your ideas off someone else. Ideas can take on a new dimension when you explain them to someone else, and input from another person can really help to motivate you.

A professional career coach may be a complete stranger who will take you through a through an initial 1:1 meeting, followed by a series of telephone calls. But you need not go to a professional. What about someone who knows you well and whose opinion you value? Maybe a relative or an old school/college/university friend? A current or previous work colleague? A neighbour? A fellow member of a sports or social club? (You will probably find it best not to use your partner in this capacity, because their personal involvement may make it difficult for them to see the wood for the trees.)

What qualities should your coach have?

- Challenging – helping you to explore alternatives not providing answers

- Good listener – you should do most of the talking
- Genuineness – someone who has a genuine interest in you
- Respect and confidentiality – both ways it is important that you talk as equals
- In touch with reality – if your dreams and goals become unrealistic your coach should bring you back to earth gently.

Remember, your coach is not your adviser. A good coach will not begin sentences with 'If I were you I would …' or 'Why don't you …?'. It is your job to develop the ideas and use your coach as a testing ground. A simple test to see whether they are the right person might be to ask yourself, 'Would I choose this person as my boss?'

When should you talk to your coach? Aim for a regular meeting for an hour or two each week or fortnight, or maybe after an initial meeting establish regular contact by phone or email.

The benefits will be that you will find that your job search plans are modified, refined, and more realistic. And all it will cost you is a special thank-you, box of chocolates or a couple of beers. ■

2

FINDING
A NEW JOB

FINDING A NEW JOB

I f you have been in employment for a long time and have not had to look for a job, you will probably find that things have changed quite a bit since you were last in this situation. To find a job you may now need to use a number of different methods, some of which may not even have existed the last time you were job-hunting. There are many ways to find a job, from networking with friends and past colleagues to using recruitment agencies, attending job fairs, searching the internet, checking the Jobcentre or looking in newspapers and magazines. You may think that you need to decide which one of the techniques you will use. However, it is best not to think of job-hunting as an 'either/or' process. The best job-hunting campaigns use *all* of the methods outlined in this chapter, because it is impossible to know which one will unearth that golden opportunity for you.

Most of the job-hunting techniques use some form of electronic communication. Many people of 50+ have excellent IT skills, of course, and if this includes you there is a fair amount in this chapter than you can skip over. But if you are new or relatively new to computers you may need to acquire or brush up skills to make sure that you do not miss out for lack of IT know-how.

If you approach your job search with an open mind and you are prepared to do some digging, you should be able to find something. The number of opportunities available today and the speed with which you can access them is quite astonishing. If you add the number of vacancies advertised on the top five UK job websites to the number of vacancies on the Jobcentre website it comes, at the time of writing, to just over 1 million. Although some jobs will be duplicated, appearing on more than one site, this is still a phenomenal number of openings. With basic computer skills you can access these opportunities with a few taps on a keyboard and a click of a mouse.

JOB OPPORTUNITIES ON THE INTERNET

'Learn IT skills. I frequently see 50+ job seekers who don't have an email address. Not only might this lead a prospective employer to think that you haven't moved with the times, but increasingly it can bar you from making an application at all, e.g. all NHS jobs are now applied for online.

'I saw a 50+ Jobseeker's Allowance [applicant] last week who needed a CV but had no idea how to use a computer. When I suggested to them that they might consider doing an IT course, for which they'd receive free tuition, they said, "Quite frankly, I'd rather be beaten with a stick."' *(Julian Hamilton, Adviser, Next Step)*

If this is *your* attitude to modern technology and you genuinely cannot see yourself using a computer, you will have problems. You might just as well put down this book and continue your job-hunt using traditional methods.

This may sound extremely harsh but the reality is that computers have become such an integral part of modern-day life that it is highly unlikely that you will find a new job that does not have at least some level of engagement with 'new' technology.

'We now face a struggle to convince everyone the net is worth using,' says Professor Richard Rose of the Oxford Internet Institute, author of a major report on internet usage. 'People who don't use the internet don't see how it will help them in their everyday affairs: for example, many older people have been educated, earned a living, shopped and paid bills for most of their lives before the internet came along', or indeed before computers became such a universal resource. Professor Rose's research shows that access to the net still varies with age: only 22 per cent of retired people surf the net, while 98 per cent of those still at school and 67 per cent of people of working age go online.

According to the Office for National Statistics Omnibus Survey 2006 an estimated 13.9 million households (57 per cent) in Great Britain could access the internet from home (January–April 2006). If you have not joined the IT revolution, now is the time to do it. You need at least basic computer skills to be able to *apply* for jobs in many organisations as well as to *do* lots of jobs, as more and more jobs require basic keyboard skills.

> Marks & Spencer recruits suitable applicants regardless of their age. People apply online through a process of talent screening. This test assesses their skills and experience against those needed for the job they are applying for. Those who pass the test are then invited for interview. The online process ensures that age is not a factor in the screening process up to this point. The company also ran training for recruiters about the new legislation, to ensure that those individuals who conduct selection interviews don't discriminate on the grounds of age. *CIPD report: Age and Recruitment. www.cipd.co.uk*

Electronic communication is no longer simply an option: it is a non-negotiable essential. Prospective employees must use the internet as part of the job search. Not only will many organisations now accept only electronic applications, there are even managers who, having received a written application, request that the same information be submitted in electronic form.

The reason for this is that electronic communications are fast, paperless and require no effort to pass on. If the personnel officer receives an electronic application from a candidate it can be quickly and effortlessly forwarded to another person. Previously, hard-copy applications had to be photocopied and then sent on through the internal mail system.

Imagine that you live in Aberdeen and you want to apply for a job in a local factory. The personnel department is located at the company's head office, in Edinburgh. You can send your electronic application to the head office in Edinburgh. The personnel department in Edinburgh can quickly scan your application to confirm that you are the kind of person the company is looking for, and with the click of a mouse they can forward your application to the recruiting manager in Aberdeen. A few years ago this process might have taken a week or more. Now it can take place in a few minutes.

'More and more organisations are insisting that candidates apply online: the NHS, Royal Mail and Essex University are three of the largest employers in this area, and all have moved over to online recruitment. It's necessary to learn at least the basics of using a computer. Some older people refuse to even try and are missing out on the opportunity to get the kind of job they may be looking for.' *(Sandra Culham, Centre Manager, Sign Post)*

Just as the internet can help you enormously in your job search, email will help you contact numerous prospective employers quickly and economically – just think of the savings on stamps and stationery, and not having to buy newspapers or magazines just for the job adverts. Using search engines and visiting recruitment websites and employers' websites will help you to unearth employment opportunities of which you would otherwise have been unaware.

But a word of caution: in some ways the internet can be too quick. Many prospective employees shoot themselves in the foot through lack of attention to detail and by being impetuous in their rush to rattle off an application.

This section looks at how you can make the most of the internet, from how to gain access to a computer, to setting up an email account and using email to best advantage, to how to surf the net to find and apply for jobs.

COMPUTER SKILLS FOR JOB SEEKERS

'It's like another language' ... If expressions such as 'search engine' and 'website', not to mention 'Google', are unfamiliar, do not be alarmed. Although it can seem that people who work with computers speak in code, you do not need to learn much of the language. However, it helps to understand the most common terms. For example, the internet (or 'net') and the World Wide Web are used interchangeably.

People of over 50 who acquire computer skills, maybe for the first time, are sometimes referred to as 'silver surfers', and many websites cater for their interests, as you will find if you put 'silver surfers' into Google or another search engine.

For the purposes of job-hunting, you will need to have four key skills:

- using a web browser (a software program that allows you to gain entry to and use the internet)
- using an internet search engine (to search for jobs and to explore employers' websites)
- basic word-processing (to write a CV and covering email letter about why you are applying for the job)
- using email (to contact recruiters).

Although this list may appear a little daunting, once you get stuck in you will find that using a computer can be great fun. Within a couple of weeks of 'logging on' for the first time, you will be looking back wondering what you were so nervous about.

If you *still* think you can get away without using a computer in your job search, think for a moment about the countless TV home improvement programmes that have shown how a little work and investment can make a previously difficult-to-sell property much more attractive to buyers. By the same token, if you are prepared to invest the effort in learning the IT skills, and possibly to acquire a computer, you will make yourself much more appealing to potential employers.

Lots of organisations can help you to take first steps to becoming familiar with computer. Possibilities include learndirect (see box), your local college or your local library. If you know anyone – children, grand-children, nephews, nieces, a friend or neighbour – who is a regular user of computers (and among those of school age that is 98 per cent), ask for help: most people will be happy to give it.

LEARNDIRECT

Learndirect is a nationwide e-learning network that has enabled millions of people throughout the UK to access learning and acquire new skills. It grew from Ufi, the 'university for industry' that was set up in 1998, and has three main strands: courses, business and advice. Since 2000, more than two million learners have gained new skills, new confidence and new opportunities with learndirect. Some 200,000 businesses have used learndirect to improve the skills of their workforce, and more than 30 million advice sessions have been provided through the online and telephone advice services.

'Generally, older people do adapt well to new technology but are often reluctant to emphasise this at interview. They sometimes prefer to underplay their skills to avoid raising expectations and avoiding disappointments.' *(Paul Toomer, Director, West Midlands Employer Coalition)*

TIPS FOR NEW COMPUTER USERS

- Be patient – everyone has difficulties and frustrations when learning about computers.
- Computers can enhance your life. Think first: what would I like to do better, do easier, or do more of in my life? Then ask someone for advice on how the computer can help you achieve that goal.
- Be selective about whom you listen to. Those who are negative about computers may be scared themselves. Do not let your enthusiasm be dampened by them.
- Go at your own pace – do not compare yourself with others. Everyone has different backgrounds and experience and everyone learns to use computers at a different pace.
- Set yourself small, realistic goals. It is better to find one useful website, or send one short email, than end up with a head full of instructions and no outcome.
- Practice makes perfect – do not be shy of repeating the things you learn time and time again until you feel you have got it. Do not be scared to make mistakes.
- Don't panic! It will all make sense in the end. You will get there. Perseverance makes experts of us all.

FIRST STEPS: EMAIL

You absolutely must, must, *must* have an email account if you are to be taken seriously as a candidate in this day and age. It says that you are living in today's world.

Look at it from a practical point of view. You are a recruiter looking to fill a vacancy quickly. You receive two applications: a beautifully presented CV and letter of application in paper form, and the second an application equally well presented in electronic form via email. Both candidates appear to be equally qualified, but one has no computer skills. In all honesty, which candidate would you invite for interview first?

To gain access to the internet and to start using email there are two things you will need. The first is a computer and the second is a subscription to an ISP, or internet service provider. Computers come in all shapes and sizes, but even basic computers can now perform word-processing tasks, access the internet and do everything you need to succeed in your job search.

Of course you can carry out your job search using the internet without going to the expense of buying a computer. By setting up your own email account with an ISP you can access emails from any computer – from a friend's computer, say, or one in an internet café or library. But ideally, if you can afford it, you should take the next step forward and buy a computer of your own.

Do not be put off by the fact that you may know little about how computers work. Think about it: how much do you know about what goes on underneath the bonnet of your car? Most people know very little, but it does not stop them driving around in cars. By the same token, you do not have to know how to build a computer in order to use it.

First let us look at setting up an email account.

There are two different ways to access email.

You can use an email program such as Microsoft Outlook or Outlook Express, or Apple Mail if you use a Mac. The messages will be stored on your hard disk. Alternatively, you can opt for web-based email.

Web-based email uses an internet browser such as Microsoft's Windows Explorer or Firefox (Firefox or Safari, if you use a Mac) and the facilities of a website provider. Your messages are stored on the server (computer) of your web provider, but can only be accessed by you using passwords. Most free email services are web-based. Setting up a web-based email account usually means that you simply need to have access to the internet.

You could have both, so that when you are travelling you can access your web-based email from an internet café.

Once you have your ISP account, you can practise using email by contacting friends and family, surf the net to find information on your hobbies and interests. The more you 'play' the more comfortable you will become.

FINDING A JOB ON THE INTERNET

Recruitment advertising is big business. Whereas it can cost thousands of pounds to advertise a job in a national daily paper, internet advertising is much more affordable for employers, and can give them greater reach. That is why there has been such an explosion of recruitment websites (or job boards, as they are sometimes called).

Magazines and newspapers now carry their recruitment advertising both in print and on their websites, which is an added bonus if you are a job seeker, as you can read the job adverts in the comfort of your home without the expense of buying the newspaper or magazine. There are many thousands of internet recruitment websites, and it can be confusing knowing where to begin. Some are listed in chapter 7, together with links to the websites of national and local newspapers, and some magazines and journals.

A number of online recruitment agencies traditionally focused on helping the more mature job seeker (some are listed in chapter 7), and it would still be worth doing a search using terms such as 'age', 'employment', 'recruitment', '50+' etc. to find them.

One of the largest recruitment websites is that of Reed (see overleaf), which has hundreds of thousands of jobs at any one time.

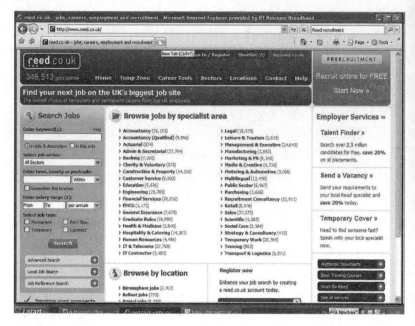

Monster (www.monster.co.uk) (see below) is a another large, and user-friendly, website which contains useful information (on finding a job and career-planning, for example).

Recruitment websites can help you in your job search in a number of ways:

- you can search for jobs by specific industry, job type or location
- you can set up a job search agent so that every time a job matching your search criteria becomes available you receive an email
- you can access the wealth of free advice on these sites
- you can join online communities and share tips with others
- you can 'post' your CV on the website – if you do this, remember to make a small change to your CV every weekend. Employers search for the 'freshest' CVs and if yours has not been refreshed for a while it will get overlooked.

EMPLOYER WEBSITES

Do not overlook employers' websites in your job search. About three-quarters of employers post their vacancies on their own websites.

To find out names of employers in your area put '[name of your town] businesses' into a search engine, such as Google, and you will get numerous sites with directories of your local organisations; then, with a little drilling-down, you will reach the vacancies pages of your local employers.

Employers' websites will often give you excellent careers advice on how to go about applying to them and will give you an idea of the kinds of jobs that are available. For an excellent example have a look at the NHS recruitment website, www.nhscareers.nhs.uk, and click 'explore by who you are' (see overleaf).

Chapter 7 includes a link to the 'Age Positive' government website, via which you can find the names employers and organisations that have demonstrated their commitment to tackling age discrimination and promoting age diversity in the workplace. If an employer is not on the list it does not mean that applications from older people are not welcomed, but the organisations listed have made a positive statement about diversity.

The NHS is the UK's largest employer, with 1.3 million employees. It has produced a range of information for managers that includes: a briefing document on why organisations need an age diversity policy; … a legislation update; … a document on how organisations must produce age profiles for applicants and those offered positions … [and] an age legislation checklist … on how to be compliant. [It also] advises trusts to adopt practices such as age awareness training. *CIPD report: Age and Recruitment. www.cipd.co.uk*

ASDA is one of the largest food retailers in the UK with approximately 150,000 employees of which 3,500 are over 65. ASDA is supportive of older workers and offers a number of flexible working practices, including grandparents' leave and carers' leave. Store managers work closely with the community to attract older workers: for example, by talking to over-50s clubs. *CIPD report: Age and Recruitment. www.cipd.co.uk*

JOBCENTRES

Many employers and recruitment agencies place their vacancies with the local Jobcentre, where there is no charge for advertising, before posting them on the internet or spending money on newspaper advertising.

Years ago the Jobcentre (previously known as the Labour Exchange) had an image of being only for low-paid unemployed people. But things have changed enormously. Indeed, if you do not include a visit to your local Jobcentre as part of your job search strategy you could miss out. Also, you do not have to be unemployed to use its services..

At the Jobcentre you can use Jobpoints, which are user-friendly touch-screens, to find information on some 400,000 vacancies held in the job bank. Jobpoints are as easy to use as a cashpoint machine.

You can access the same information through the Jobcentre's website (see chapter 7).

New Deal is a special programme available through the Jobcentre offering personal advice and a wide range of support to help people find a job. It could be useful if you have been finding it difficult either to get a job or to get one that pays a decent wage. For more information about New Deal and whether you are eligible for the programme visit your local Jobcentre or www.newdeal.gov.uk.

RECRUITMENT AGENCIES

Just as estate agents earn their fees when they sell a house, recruitment agencies earn their fees when they place a candidate in a job. So it is in the recruitment agencies' interests to have you on their books. Even so, the reality is that many agencies tend to favour younger clients. One older job applicant, a chartered accountant, was told by an agency he visited that he looked 50, not 70, therefore employment should not be a problem – but the agency never got back to him.

Another problem is that many agency staff rely very heavily on computerised matching of skills to job requirements. They tend to be uncomfortable with clients who want to change direction, particularly those who want to move to a lower-level job, and they are less adept at assessing transferable skills. None the less, you will need to engage with recruitment agencies. The ones you register with will depend on what kind of job you are looking for: local, national, industry specialist, or 'executive search', the latter being agencies that specialise in senior-level recruitment. A quick search of the newspaper or your professional journal will help you to identify which agency to contact. Follow up with a telephone call. Note that while some agencies welcome spec-ulative applications/CVs so that they can add them to a database, others prefer only to receive applications for specific vacancies.

If you are invited to interview by an agency, treat it in the same way as you would treat an interview with an employer. The employer has entrusted the recruitment agency with the job of doing the 'first sift', and if you do not make a good impression you will be out of the race.

'I am now in the midst of a mid-life career change. I want to "downsize", but am finding it a struggle. I have come up against major hurdles stemming from the matching process [of transferable skills to job requirements], and find that professional recruiters tend not to know of employers who value the experience of older employees or how to exploit transferable skills.

'Mid-life downsizes are not considered a marketable commodity in an employment environment that is becoming increasingly dominated by the recruitment industry.

'As matching becomes increasingly "technologised" by the industry it also becomes simplified and standardised, with an over-emphasis on direct experience and age-linked positions – and an under-awareness of the value of transferable skills.

'The transferable skill problem is most acute in relation to skill levels and the inability of [many recruiters] to identify where higher-skilled candidates, working in a job they enjoy, can add real value.' *(male professional, 55)*

'If applicants have low self-esteem or lack confidence following bad experiences, they should find a professional recruitment agency that will work with them on interview technique and help them prepare. Equally, arrogance and an "I know more than you do" attitude is a sure-fire way to de-select yourself. Look to agencies that have the Diversity Assured standard from the REC/C2E or other diversity quality marks for assistance.' *(professional recruiter)*

JOB FAIRS

Recruitment events are sometimes occupation-specific: for example, aimed at graduates, geared to the IT sector, or focused on a particular town or city. Do not miss out on the opportunity to attend a job fair, even if they are recruiting people from a completely different specialism. For example, if you are a chef and there is a graduate recruitment fair in town, go along anyway.

Dress as you would if you were attending a job interview and make sure you have an ample supply of CVs with you. Wander around the room to get a feel for who is recruiting and when you have identified your target organisations visit their stands. As an introduction, ask the people who are manning the stand to tell you a little more about their organisation – let them do the talking first. Remember, employers attend recruitment fairs to 'sell' their organisation and to recruit talent. You could well find that you are in conversation with the HR manager, and just because the HR manager has come to recruit graduates this does not mean that they have forgotten that they need to recruit a chef for the staff restaurant. The other alternative is to submit a written application along with the other 72 applicants, but here you are standing in front of the recruiter 'being interviewed'. Yes, it is a long-shot, but being bold and proactive in this way can pay off. Be prepared for a short interview; at recruitment fairs they often have little booths so that employers can do a quick pre-interview screen. If you are in luck you might just get invited to a formal interview.

NETWORKING YOUR WAY TO A JOB

Networking is a proactive method of building and maximising relationships to help you to advance your career. Networking is equally effective whether you are job-hunting, seeking to rise up the corporate ladder, or striking out as an independent. It also works for self-employed people and interim workers.

Your network becomes increasingly important as you get older. Some people believe that as few as 25 per cent of jobs are ever advertised and that about 50 per cent of people over 40 find work through personal contacts. Some people network quite naturally, while for others the very thought of it makes them feel uncomfortable.

DEVELOPING A NETWORKING STRATEGY

'Ninety-nine per cent of advertising doesn't sell much of anything.' (David Ogilvy, advertising industry guru)

The success rate for networking is no better and may be even worse. But when it does work, it can bring powerful rewards. Just as the gardener reaps rewards for working and improving the soil, you will gain rewards from your networking activities.

Look at the table opposite and decide which methods you will use to develop your network.

NETWORKING WORKS

In many fields, networking is almost part of the job description. For example, for freelance workers and consultants, networking helps to establish, expand and constantly refresh the field of contacts.

You can network using internet forums, attending or speaking at seminars, conferences or charity events, joining business networking

PLACES/OPPORTUNITIES FOR BUILDING A NETWORK

Mentor someone or ask someone to mentor you	Attend conferences and seminars
Call one person a day whom you would like to talk to but who is not on your priority list	Allow one evening a month for a drink after work with a friend or colleague that you do not see enough of
Get involved in task forces or other exercises	Give some of your time to charity
Send reports of your work to others who may be interested	Subscribe and contribute to online networks
Attend external networking or speed-networking events	Make time for meeting the occasional supplier
Talk to others about what they are doing in areas which may be of interest	Write papers, articles (or even a book) for general publication
Plan regular reviews to talk about your performance and your development with your boss	Present at external events such as professional institute branch meetings or become a committee member
Offer to present at meetings or conferences and bring others in to talk at yours	Attend training courses internally and externally
Do a regular report on you and your team's exercises and send it to the people who might want to know	When you dig out useful information, think about who else might find it interesting, and forward it on

clubs, or writing articles for trade journals and inviting feedback (views, comments, questions).

You could also try 'speed networking'. First, use Google or another search engine to find our about local events. Then develop your own 'sales pitch' – a memorable vignette that says who you are and what you do, and which you can communicate in a couple of minutes. Attend the events you have selected, and be prepared: take lots of business cards with you and also a notepad, so that you jot down names of people to whom you have spoken and any information you have gathered (you could go so far as to develop your own scoring system in advance). At the event, never be fooled by appearances – for all you know, the unshaven, scruffily dressed young guy who arrived late could be the owner of a significant local business.

Building a network doesn't happen in a day. All of the methods work, but you cannot do them all at once, so choose two or three – and do it now.

NETWORKING TACTICS TO FIND WORK

If you are looking for a new job right now, you probably do not have time for many of the long-term strategic methods. But networking can help and is far more powerful than scanning 'situations vacant' and searching websites.

Networking is not about pestering people nor is it about embarrassing them so that they feel morally obliged to help you or even give you a job. Networking is about approaching people genuinely to ask for advice and ideas on how you can get your next job: You are not writing to them, telephoning or meeting them for a job. This is extremely important. When you make it quite clear that what you want from them is advice and ideas (not a job), you will find them far more forthcoming.

Just look at the power of numbers. Imagine you start off with the top 15 people in your network (see page 56), you contact them and they each give you the names of two of their contacts. That is an extra 30 people, so you now have a network of 45 – and so it can go on.

It is not difficult to have 40 or 50 (or more) people helping you in your job search. People like to have their ego stroked by being asked for advice and most people will help if they are asked. But if it appears that you are asking for a job, you will embarrass them.

You also need to avoid embarrassing yourself. After all, broadcasting that you are on the dole is not a great ego-booster. So how are you going to say it? Some people find it very difficult to tell others that they are looking for work, but if you can overcome this barrier quickly you will be able to start networking straight away.

Write down why you are looking for work. Do not be self-effacing and do not be critical of your (previous) employer. Now say it four or five times out loud. The 'bottom line' is still the same, but you should now feel a lot more comfortable in explaining to other people why you are looking for work and why you are asking for their help and advice.

Go through your address book, diary, business card file, customer records, correspondence files, etc. and brainstorm. Write down the names and contact details of people you know. At this point include anyone and everyone you can think of: for example, friends, work colleagues, fellow club members, consultants, doctors, dentist, solicitor, bank manager, accountant, neighbours, customers, suppliers, professional contacts, competitors, university/college/school friends, past employers and colleagues, relatives, teachers. Ask your partner and close friends for ideas. There – you have started networking.

You can also develop 'virtual' contacts through internet chat rooms and forums and through specialised networking websites – details and links in chapter 7.

Now you have your network, follow this plan of campaign:

- identify and prioritise whom you should contact first. Go for people whom you can contact relatively easily. Aim high – the higher up the organisation the better. People who could potentially employ you are even better. People on the same level but in a different function who can 'pass you on' to their peer are also useful. (However, people on the same level/in the same function may see you as a competitor.) If your intention is to become self-employed, your previous employer could be the one to get you off the starting blocks by giving you some freelance work.

■ now choose the top 15 names on your list and contact them. Decide which approach will be best. As a general principle: first choice is to see them in person; second is to telephone; third is to write a letter; and the least favoured option is to send an email. Remember, your objective is not simply to inform people of the fact that you are looking for work. You want to motivate them to do something to help you. The more personal your contact, the more likely it is to succeed. Of course, there are exceptions. If you are working in the Netherlands and have a friend in Japan who might be able to help you to get a job in California, email might work. But then again it might not. Email is excellent for maintaining business contacts and exchanging information, but as a starting point for network development it is not a good method.

Whatever you do, get to the point quickly. Don't waste their time. Achieve your three objectives:

■ to let them know you are looking for work – so that they can keep their eyes and ears open;
■ to ask them for the names of two of their contacts whom you might approach;
■ to ask for their advice about opportunities/recruitment consultants/ journals/advertisements they might have seen.

Remember, you get only one opportunity to make a first impression. The most powerful 'in' you can get is a personal introduction. Do not over-stretch yourself by using the blunderbuss technique. If you try to contact everyone in your network on day 1 you will not be able to handle the workload.

Keep prioritising and manage the project – for example, by following up with a phone call if you have said you will. Whenever you have made contact with someone in your network, send a short thank-you note, or an email. It costs little and shows genuine appreciation.

Networking is contrived, conscious and proactive – and none the worse for it.

> 'Shakespeare wrote his sonnets within a strict discipline, fourteen lines of iambic pentameter, rhyming in three quatrains and a couplet. Were his sonnets dull? Mozart wrote his sonatas within an equally rigid discipline – exposition, development, and recapitulation. Were they dull?' *(David Ogilvy, advertising industry guru)*

SUGGESTED NETWORKING TECHNIQUE

Do you know anyone – a neighbour, a friend, a cousin, a friend of a friend – who works in an organisation to which you are applying? Save yourself the price of a stamp and ask them if they would be kind enough to take your application into work and give it to the person who is recruiting. If someone is prepared to do this for you, they are effectively giving you a referral, and your application could well end up way ahead of others.

> 'Think about doing voluntary work to increase your current work skills. Attend learndirect and engage in enhancing your basic skills in literacy and numeracy if this is an area that needs support. Consider looking at part-time work or job-share options to enable you to gain confidence.' *(Sue Gaskell, Pertemps People Development Group)*

VOLUNTARY WORK

If you are having difficulty finding a job, voluntary work could offer the opportunity you need to break the vicious circle of not being able to get a job because you do not have the right skills and experience – and not being able to get those skills and experience because you have no job.

Voluntary work is a great way of getting into a working environment while helping others. It is also a good way of keeping your skills up to date or learning new ones, and boosting your CV. When you write your CV you can include your voluntary work under 'Professional experience', bring your career up to date and demonstrate your commitment.

Doing voluntary work can have a number of other benefits:

- you can explore career interests
- you will widen your network, which could lead to a job opportunity
- you will boost your confidence, by giving yourself a sense of purpose and adding some routine to your life.

Volunteering opportunities can encompass anything from working in a charity shop to doing admin, staffing events, being a driver, trainer, team leader – there are openings all the way up to non-executive director level.

Are you prepared to make a full-time commitment for a fixed term? Have you ever considered volunteering overseas but ruled it out because you thought you were too old or could not commit enough time? If so, you may be able to think again. Over the past five years, according to David Stitt, managing director of Gap Year for Grown-ups, a company that provides career breaks and voluntary work opportunities in many countries, 'it has become far safer – and more professionally acceptable – to take up a job volunteering overseas'.

You may be able to get a contract working overseas for a development or humanitarian charity such as VSO (Voluntary Service Overseas) or Médecins Sans Frontières (MSF). People working for these organisations are usually paid a very low subsistence allowance. Accommodation and flights are also paid for and you will be placed where your skills are needed most. The jobs available are usually highly demanding – no longer are people flown half-way across the world to help dig drainage ditches.

Charities need people with skills that can be put to good use on their overseas projects. Volunteers who come back testify to increased self-confidence, an improved CV and a more positive outlook.

See chapter 7 for links to places that offer volunteer work.

'Show that you are willing and able to learn new skills. The best way to demonstrate this is to have a recent relevant qualification in your CV.

'The single best way to enhance your employment prospects is to have achieved some kind of IT qualification, which the majority of employers now value more highly than the possession of a full clean driving licence. IT skills/qualifications also assist in finding and applying for jobs.

'Another way to show ability and willingness and to gain valuable experience is to do some voluntary work. Usually there's plenty to choose from (e.g. on www.do-it.org.uk).

'Make applications and CVs as relevant to the job being applied for as possible and never miss the opportunity to sell yourself.' *(Julian Hamilton, Adviser, Next Step)*

TRAINING AND RE-TRAINING

There are very few jobs (if any) that require minimal or no skills at all, and as technology advances the need for people with a wide variety of skills, including IT skills, increases. The management guru Peter Drucker predicted that 'the factories of the future will have only two employees: a person and a dog. The person's job will be to feed the dog and the dog's job will be to bite the person if they touch any of the controls or switches'.

This may be an exaggeration, but it offers an insight into the way the world of work is changing. Think about the developments and technological advances that have taken place, at home and at work, over the past two or three decades. When did you last see a typewriter? Do you still use a film camera? Whatever happened to the blackboard in the school classroom? Technological advances mean that new skills are constantly needed in the workplace. Training and re-training are the key to learning new skills and unlocking your own potential.

If you are having difficulty finding a new job it may be that you need a skills makeover. You can take control of your future by deciding to improve your skills. Your chances of getting work, gaining a promotion, improving your career, starting your own business or even being paid a higher salary will all be improved if you develop your skills.

Fortunately, help is at hand. Through learndirect you can gain access to almost a million courses country-wide in subjects from mountain survival to catering.

Have you decided on a complete change of direction? Re-training could give you an opportunity for a completely different career. Have a look at jobs where there are skills shortages, such as the traditional building trades – there seems to be a shortage of plumbers and electricians in many areas and their earnings are very healthy. Or what about IT? Age should be no barrier to re-training as a web developer, for example, which would guarantee you an income for as long as you wish to continue working.

You will find information on options for training and re-training in chapter 7, as well as on the internet.

A word of caution: be wary of organisations that purport to offer IT courses with a pot of gold at the end of the rainbow. These companies charge you a substantial fee up-front for a training course with an 'offer of guaranteed employment' at the end. There have been stories of people paying for courses leading to qualifications that mean nothing to employers, and certainly not ending up with a job.

Check that the course you will study has a market value: for example, you cannot go too far wrong with Microsoft Certified Courses. Check out the level of support the organisation can give you in finding a job (and its success rates). Some have their own recruitment agency: that way they get a recruitment fee for placing you with an employer – and you get straight into a job. ∎

'We think it's a myth that older workers are less prepared to learn. It certainly isn't a trend here.'
(Elaine Bromberg, Diversity Manager, HSBC plc)

3

APPLYING FOR A JOB

APPLYING FOR A JOB

'Work is the true elixir of life. The busiest man is the happiest man. Excellence in any art or profession is attained only by hard and persistent work. Never believe that you are perfect. When a man imagines, even after years of striving, that he has attained perfection, his decline begins.' *(Sir Theodore Martin, poet, translator and biographer, on reaching the age of 92)*

Your job application is your entrée to the world of work and your first opportunity to sell your skills and achievements to your prospective employer. It may seem obvious, but where job applications are concerned the importance of attention to detail cannot be over-emphasised. Yet, amazingly, people commonly commit 'candidate suicide' by making stupid mistakes in their job applications or CVs. For example, well qualified applicants who get the name of the organisation to which they are applying wrong are likely to go straight on to the 'no' pile. Sometimes people copy and paste the content of a previous letter of application, and forget to change the addressee's name. Others make typographical errors, or apply online but forget to attach their CV.

And this trend is if anything strengthening. Applications are actually becoming sloppier, probably because email is so fast that many people fail to check things as thoroughly as they should. This chapter will look at how you can make winning applications.

Before that, let us have a look at some of the other things people do that qualify as 'candidate suicide', both in their initial applications and at interview. Some of them make amusing reading, but they are all sad stories, because every one of them represents a lost opportunity: a job application that was unsuccessful because of an avoidable mistake.

CANDIDATE SUICIDE: HOW TO COMMIT IT

A recent internet search revealed the following listings on websites and postings on blogs:

- a candidate who gave her email address as grumpy_grandma@domain.com. (Lesson: if you use a fun email address or a family email address such as thewaltonsfamily@waltonsmountain.com keep it for personal emails and register a different email address for your job search)
- someone called Brian who sent his CV out with his name spelled BrAln, and wondered why he had had no responses to his applications after two months. (Lesson: check, check and check again. Do not rely on your spellchecker to pick up errors)
- a job applicant whose cover letter said he was sending it to the HR director as a 'courtesy' before 'making any attempt to sidestep their authority and going directly to the 'real decision-maker'. (Lesson: trying to be smart in job applications is likely to backfire on you)
- an applicant who said their CV was posted to a particular website from which the recruiter should download it. The recruiter, naturally, did not bother. (Lesson: you need to make things easy for the recruiter, not make work for them)

The Chartered Institute of Personnel and Development, Europe's largest organisation for human resource professionals, has provided further examples:

- a CV in connection with a quality control technician vacancy listed, under key skills, 'attenshion to detail'
- a candidate wrote that in January 2207 she would be

doing an NVQ Level 3 in Customer Service. Formidable forward planning . . .

Some of the CIPD's examples were from interviews, including the preliminary telephone interviews which are often carried out by recruiters in advance of face-to-face ones:

- during a telephone interview for a prospective IT trainer, the interviewer, concerned that an applicant was a 'techie' who thought he could train, asked what his preferred learning style was. His reply was 'I tell them what button to press in what order and the information required for each data field'
- another telephone interviewee, when asked what he thought of multiple intelligence theory, said, 'Well, some people have learning problems and we need to take account of their needs.' (Lesson: every field has its own jargon, and it is there for a reason: if you claim to be in that field, be sure you are up to speed)
- a candidate for a job within the airport retail sector, which experiences quiet periods between flights, was asked what he would do to keep himself busy during these times; his reply was 'plug in my iPod and read a magazine'
- an interviewee for a fundraising post gabbled incoherently at great speed, interrupted the interviewers several times and kept sniffing. He had slightly suspicious-looking white marks on his nose ('We found a foil wrap in the gents where he had been prior to interview')
- an interviewee for an admin job that involved creating and updating spreadsheets and databases was asked about his IT skills; he went on to describe (albeit rather vaguely) a spreadsheet he had created in his current role. 'All became clear when we asked the very next candidate the same question and he went on to talk in much more detail about

the same spreadsheet: they were colleagues both under threat of redundancy in their existing roles and the first chap had clearly decided to pinch the second chap's spreadsheet as an example'

- an interviewee who, when asked at the end of the interview for details of referees, said she did not watch football

- a candidate for a project manager's post, asked which aspect of project management he did not like, replied 'change'

- a young man, asked what retailing experience he had had, answered, 'I have sold doughnuts for a day' (the company with the job opening was 'a very high-profile department store offering high-quality merchandise and customer service')

- a candidate for a deputy post answered every question put to him by first repeating the question, exam-style

- an applicant for senior manager post, asked how he would deal with a difficult staff member, said that he would dismiss them on the spot

- a candidate for an electrician's job, who qualified for one respondent's worst-ever interview, made it clear from the start he had a problem with women (the respondent, and lead interviewer, was female): 'When I asked him a question, he replied to the man I was interviewing with. Halfway through, he started picking a scab on the side of his face. It started pouring with blood. He promptly wiped the blood off with his finger and licked it clean.'

Even when the recruitment process is complete, some candidates will not accept the recruiter's decision gracefully:

- 'We have had a couple of instances where rejected candidates have felt the need to write and complain that they were not given the job. One who had applied for a part-time sales adviser position felt that as she had a degree (with honours) there was no doubt in her mind that she should have been offered the position, as "it's only retail, after all". She sent her letter to the CEO!'

■ another unsuccessful candidate was most put out that she had been interviewed by a young lady who was Spanish, and asked to be re-interviewed by someone who was English as she felt this was why she had not got the job.

In addition to the above, the CIPD respondents cited numerous examples of candidates who:

■ made no eye contact during the entire interview
■ made sexist comments
■ had no idea what the company did.

All of these represent lost opportunities for someone to get a job. The UK may currently have a skills shortage and employers are keen to employ talented people, but they are not desperate. If a candidate cannot be bothered to make the effort when they should be trying to make a good impression, why should anyone think they would do so as an employee?

While the examples given above illustrate what *not* to do during the job application process, the rest of this chapter will show how you can create a positive impression.

CVS AND APPLICATION LETTERS/EMAILS

Your CV and introductory letter or email will have a strong influence on whether or not you get an interview. The decision between a 'no', a 'regret, but hold' (you are not exactly what we are looking for at present but we will keep your details on file) and an 'invite for interview' can be made in as little as 30 seconds.

LETTERS OF APPLICATION

Your immaculately presented CV and beautifully written letter of application, or the application form that took you two hours to write, can be scanned by a recruiter and a decision made in less than a minute. The recruiter first filters out all of the people who do not match the selection criteria, keeping the people who do. When you apply online you may well find that your application is scanned by software to find 'keywords'. If they are not there you may receive an automatic 'thank-you but no thank-you' response, and that rejection could be triggered just because you typed 'ProductManager' instead of 'Product Manager', and ignored your mistake when you ran the spellchecker.

> 'You'll reduce your chances if your CV and covering letter are too old-fashioned and your supporting statement overflows with details of every job undertaken but is not specific to the job description.' *(Sandra Culham, Centre Manager, Sign Post)*

Your application letter or email is usually the first thing an employer sees, so it is important that it makes a positive impression. Here are some things to bear in mind when writing the letter.

- Use a powerful opening sentence, perhaps along the lines of: *'I would like to apply for the position of administration supervisor as I believe that I have the qualities which you have outlined in your advertisement.'*
- Introduce your three top skills or qualities which match you to the job – but do not re-write your CV. For more advice on how to do this, see below
- Because the letter is all about you it is easy to find yourself starting every sentence with 'I' – but try very hard to avoid this

- Make your letter the right length – more than just a couple of sentences, but no more than one page
- Be precise – make sure you refer to the job title and quote the reference in the introduction to the letter: the recruiter could be recruiting for a number of similar positions
- Be formal and not over-familiar. Do not address the person you are approaching by their first name
- Make the application letter specific to the job. With word-processing it so easy to do this and there is just no excuse for bland, one-size-fits-all letters. What these say is that the applicant cannot be bothered to write something tailored to the specific vacancy and employing organisation. Use key phrases from the job advertisement in the letter and refer to the strongest, most relevant achievements listed in your CV
- Present the letter well, in the same font as your CV. If you are using the postal system, print it on to white A4 paper; enclose your letter and CV in a quality white envelope and use a first-class stamp (one personnel manager admits that she once had so many applications for a secretarial job that she rejected all applications in brown envelopes or bearing second-class stamps)
- Use the spellchecker and then, for good measure, ask a friend to proofread your letter and CV
- End on a positive statement of what you can bring to the organisation and how you look forward to hearing from them
- Unless specifically asked to do so, do not send a handwritten letter
- End the letter with 'Yours sincerely' if you are writing to 'Dear Mr/Ms [name]', or 'Yours faithfully' for 'Dear Sir/Madam' – and do not forget to sign it.

Most of these principles also apply to emails, but in addition bear the following in mind:

- Do not be in too much of a hurry to press 'send'. Make sure you have checked and re-checked the spelling and grammar, and make sure you have written full words in formal English
- Your email address can present you in an unprofessional light. If yours is grumpy_grandpa@thepub.com or linda@shopstilldrops.com, get another one for your job search and keep the fun one for friends and family. You can open a free email address at many sites, including Yahoo or Google's gmail
- Be specific in the subject line: for example, 'Job application: Distribution Centre Manager – ref Ch/276'. Do not try to be clever, cryptic or amusing
- Make sure your attachments are accessible and can be opened by the recipient: most can read MS Word, and all can read .txt documents
- The content should read like a cover letter – because that is what it is, and it has to do the same selling job
- In emails, never use emoticons, such as (-: This is a formal business communication, not a message to one of your pals
- Before you click 'send', do make sure that you have attached your CV, that it is the correct version, and that it is not entitled Bill's CV version 783 (which suggests that your level of success with other applications has not been that high).

It is as well to be aware that, despite the Age Regulations that came into force in October 2006, discrimination on grounds of age has not been stamped out and there is no shortage of evidence that ageist principles are still applied at application stage, as well as later in the recruitment process. Linked to the issue of age are assumptions that someone in mid-life or older will want a high salary to reflect their qualifications and experience. Such assumptions are discrimina-tory in themselves and can be a particular drawback if you are trying to change your career direction. Addressing the issue in your letter of application, perhaps by saying that you fully appreciate that you would be working at a lower level, and for a lower salary, than you have previously, could help you overcome this kind of knee-jerk reaction.

> 'I kept being told I was over-qualified. I sent out numerous applications and haven't been offered one interview. One of the arguments used against hiring someone over 50 is that I wouldn't be happy with the money on offer. This is ridiculous, because if I was not happy with the salary I wouldn't be applying for the job.' *(professional woman, 53, seeking to change career)*

> 'Being "over-qualified" has been the most common issue that I have come across, along with being interviewed by younger people who feel threatened by my experience.' *(senior marketing professional, female, 48)*

It is also as well to be aware that people who have previously been employed at director level or run their own business face a particularly tough challenge when trying to find employment, even if they more than satisfy all the skills and experience requirements, because they are likely to be seen as a threat by younger, less qualified managers.

A very senior auditor, who had also run his own auditing business, found it very difficult to find a job at the age of 54. Eventually he found a temporary one, two grades below his previous job, where he felt 'humiliated' because he was answerable to someone with 14 years' less experience than himself.

For people in a similar position, self-employment (see chapter 6) could be a better option.

Those who have run their own companies as sole traders or in partnership may find that the skills and experience they accumulated in that role count for little with agencies and employers because there is little or no formal training or qualification underpinning it. If this is an issue for you, taking a few courses, possibly with learndirect (see page 42), could help to improve your chances of employment.

TOP TIPS FOR OLDER JOB APPLICANTS

Look for jobs where there is a specific requirement for experience.

- Stress your *levels* of experience and ensure that your CV *sells* your skills and experience.
- Get some basic computer skills if you have none.
- Emphasise positive points, e.g. loyalty, and no problems with childcare responsibilities.
- Stress the absence of domestic crises potential as you have no small children. Stress your flexibility concerning leave requirements and working hours.
- Keep an open mind about learning new skills, e.g. enrol on open learning courses to acquire computer skills or improve basic skills (if required) or just check on what courses are available via these centres. For example, short courses in health and safety, or first aid in the workplace, are often available. *(John Davis, Regional Employer Engagement Team, Jobcentre Plus)*

MATCHING SKILLS AND EXPERIENCE TO THE JOB

To do this you will need a copy of the job description, a document that states the duties, level of decision-making responsibility, reporting lines and performance indicators (how you will be assessed in the job).

You may need to request this document from the organisation. If no job description exists, ask yourself why not. There may be a good reason, or it may be that the employer has not yet decided what the duties will be (which could be potential source of future conflict), or it may well be that the organisation has an informal structure and culture, and your job description may simply be 'whatever is needed to get the job done', as is often the case with small or start-up companies.

Re-read the advertisement, the application form and your CV (see below) alongside the job description, to be sure you understand what it is that the organisation is asking for. Highlight key phrases within it, then think hard about how you could demonstrate, from your own working background, your ability to match the requirements.

There is quite an art to the matching of skills and experience to the requirements of a job, and to understand fully how to do this, especially if you have been away from the job-hunting scene for a while, consider spending some time using a skills assessment toolkit such as the one produced by Fairplay and available via the TAEN (The Age and Employment Network) website: http://www.taen.org.uk/resources/individuals.htm.

This will enable you to analyse your experience objectively and identify your transferable skills – technical, managerial, strategic or interpersonal – and to show, through your achievements, how you have used them. Working through this kind of assessment is invaluable preparation for interviews, too, as it encourages you to look at all areas of your life, not just your paid employment, to identify what your experience of life can bring to the job in question. This might include, for example, dealing with money, communicating with people, customer service, solving problems and resolving conflict, managing projects, working within a team, managing change, or using IT.

CVS

Your CV is your greatest marketing tool. Sadly, it is not possible to give definitive advice to the effect that if you do X, Y and Z in a CV you will automatically get an interview. Recruiters have personal preferences in how they like to see CVs written, in addition to which your CV is a very personal document and in the final analysis you are the best judge of whether your CV represents you in as good a light as possible.

There is a debate as to whether photographs should be included in CVs. Most recruiters suggest that unless you are applying for a job as an actor or a model, there is no need for a photograph.

Unless the employer has asked for it, do not include your date of birth in applications (never raise potential barriers with employers). Note that there is a common misconception that it is now unlawful for an employer to ask for an applicant's date of birth. Although it is not unlawful, it may be unwise on the employer's part to ask for this information because the decision to do so could be challenged.

Stories continue to circulate about applicants sending off CVs stating their age to potential employers and being rejected (or receiving no response at all), but being invited for interview after submitting the same CV with no reference to age.

If potential employers discriminate against you on grounds of age they are acting unlawfully (age discrimination regulations have been in place since October 2006 to outlaw such practice). It is very difficult to know, and still harder to prove, that you have been de-selected because of your age, but there are steps you can take if you suspect you have fallen foul of age discrimination: see chapter 8 of *How to Recognise Cases of Age Discrimination: a guide for workers*, a publication in which Help the Aged and TAEN (The Age and Employment Network) were involved:
www.taen.org.uk/publications/ad_guide_for_workers.pdf.

It is encouraging to note that many organisations are now adopting an age-positive policy and welcome applications from mature

'Standard Jobcentre application forms do not ask for date of birth, so employers cannot sift by age. Additionally, people may wish not to include their date of birth or age on a CV. CVs should focus on skills, competencies and achievements. To increase their chances job seekers should do confidence-building and interview technique training.' *(Karol Doveston, NEPL (Able to Work Project), Jobcentre Plus Liaison Manager)*

'Make sure that your CV is skills-based and doesn't go back too far. Express your enthusiasm to learn and develop new skills in your covering letter. Emphasise how transferable your skills are. Demonstrate your ability to multi-task. Never, ever think that you are too old.

'If you are going to apply for a junior position that is a change of direction, say in the covering letter that although you expect they may have been considering a school or college leaver, just think how much more they will get in terms of work ethics and responsibility. Sometimes, pointing out the reason why you may be rejected can turn a negative into a positive. It has worked well for some of my clients.'
(Sandra Culham, Centre Manager, Sign Post)

applicants. None the less, recruitment advisers generally suggest that applicants leave their age out of their CV.

Another debate centres on whether job applicants should use a chronological CV or a functional CV. Chronological CVs are the most common. These track your career from start to present day, usually starting with your current or most recent position and taking the reader back step by step to the beginning of your working life. Use a chronological CV when the job you have applied for is a logical successor to your previous jobs. Previous jobs show that your responsibilities have increased as your experience has broadened. The chronological CV can also demonstrate a solid career history. However, this kind of CV may not be the best format for older candidates.

The functional CV or skills CV is often recommended for older applicants or for people changing career direction. The functional CV puts the emphasis on your skills and experiences without being heavily biased towards a particular job. You may also consider using a functional CV if you have worked for obscure organisations, or you want to hide the fact that you were self-employed.

You can also use a functional CV if you have had a lot of job changes, a long period of unemployment, or if there is no obvious career direction. You still give your job history, but briefly, in a separate section. A functional CV can highlight skills and attributes very effectively. However, some recruiters are very wary of functional CVs because they know that some candidates use this method to hide dark aspects of their past or a tendency to itchy feet. That said, functional CVs *can* work and can win you an interview.

See pages 78–80 for examples of a chronological CV and a functional CV so that you can see the difference. You can find other examples via a search engine such as Google and decide which style is best for you. Remember, your CV is not carved in stone. You could try different CVs with different employers to see if one seems to work better than another.

FUNCTIONAL CV

Janine Parks used a functional CV to disguise the fact that she was made redundant six months ago. Hers is not a definitive CV, but a real person's disguised for this book.

Janine Parks
76 Middle Road, North Park
Southwood AA66 77ZZ
Home tel: (0303) 30303
Email: Janine.Parks@home.oc.ku

OBJECTIVE

● To secure a senior management position within banking where my previous experience, sales, leadership and banking skills can be utilised to their full potential.

● Highly motivated, energetic senior manager who has successfully achieved objectives through developing people. A flexible leader with strong interpersonal and communication skills who thrives on being involved in leading teams in a creative environment where there is constant challenge. Responsible for results of a keenly focused team in terms of sales, quality and profitability. Displays initiative and a positive outlook to all challenges, ideas generator, decisive and highly adaptable to change. Extensive experience and knowledge of both general and sales management, with an in-depth understanding of the people business.

ACHIEVEMENTS

- Developed teams of managers monitoring both personal performance and that of the sales units, ensuring objectives achieved together with quality and service standards being maintained.
- Created a competitive team spirit whereby individual and collective performance was recognised. Provided league tables, instigated competitions, produced interesting and varied communication formats.
- Energised team, created environment ensuring national sales campaigns were tackled enthusiastically with success being achieved and measured in improving performance position. Appointed and managed new direct sales force including sales meetings, one-to-one coaching and field visits. Developed and nurtured relationships with sales units to achieve common business objectives, resulting in business levels being increased by 140 per cent over a 6-month period.
- Produced quarterly/annual business plans to ensure focus and direction to achieving business objectives
- Instigated and developed a programme and systems for achieving Total Quality Management resulting in customer service complaints being reduced by 28 per cent in three months.
- Responsible for staff recruitment at junior management level. Disciplinary matters and general personnel responsibilities, including managing staff budgets.
- Responsible for quarterly/annual appraisal process whereby individuals recognise critical success factors which are incorporated within a personal development plan.
- Involved with the training of staff both within units and at area training centre. Follow-up process adopted to ensure training benefits maximised.

CAREER HISTORY

Area Sales Manager, Blue Building Society Responsible for 16 managers, 135 staff. Reported to Area Sales Director
Regional Sales Manager, Green Bank Responsible for 8 managers, 4 direct sales staff
Regional Manager, Green Bank
Assistant Regional Manager, Green Bank
Branch Manager, Green Bank
Branch Manager, White Building Society
Junior management/senior clerical

PERSONAL DEVELOPMENT

Sundridge Park Management Centre: leadership skills development
Peters Management Consultants: sales management training
Ashridge Management College Extensive internal training covering a wide range of topics

ADDITIONAL INFORMATION

Fellow Chartered Building Society Institute
School governor/chairman of charitable trust
Computer-literate: all Microsoft Office software packages

INTERESTS

Fine wine, cooking, riding, trying to keep fit

CHRONOLOGICAL CV

NAME **Keith Jameson**
ADDRESS 14 Lakeview Road, Woodlands, Cumbria LL1 1DD
TEL. NO. 01234 5678
EMAIL Keith@lakeview.ac.ku

PERSONAL PROFILE
I am a qualified and experienced maintenance engineer, with effective communication skills and management experience in plant hire. Currently undertaking further management skills training.

EMPLOYMENT
May 1996–April 2007: Manager, Large Plant Hire Ltd, Woodlands
• Responsible for the smooth and effective management of this small but busy branch, hiring out tools and equipment to customers in the construction trade and to the public.
• Oversaw the successful introduction of a computerised stock control system.
• Developed health & safety training programme, which has been adopted nationally.
• Almost doubled turnover in spite of the difficulties experienced in the construction trade.

February 1990–May 1996: Assistant Manager, Large Plant Hire Ltd, Woodlands
• Assistant manager, responsible for deputising for manager in his absence.
• Responsible for stock control and ordering
• Reduced inventory by 25% and maintained good customer satisfaction

October 1982–February 1990: General Assistant, Plant Hire, Woodlands
• Dealt with customers who hired tools and equipment
• Responsible for checking over and maintenance of the equipment, undertaking basic repair work as necessary
• Developed communication skills, as the work involved giving instruction and advice to the customers to ensure customer safety, and correct usage of the equipment
• Attendance at various in-company health and safety training courses

September 1976–October 1982: Maintenance Assistant,
Woodlands Borough Council
• Responsible for the upkeep of machinery and tools in the Parks and Gardens Department
• Undertook simple repair work of gates, seats and other Parks equipment.

EDUCATION
1982–4   Woodlands College: BTEC Engineering Maintenance
1974–6   Woodlands College: City & Guilds General Horticulture
1969–74 Woodlands School: GCE Metalwork, History and English

OTHER INFORMATION
• Since being made redundant due to a company takeover and closure of the branch, I have sought to improve my management skills. I am currently taking an NEBSM Certificate in Supervisory Management course at Woodlands College
• I hold a clean driving licence.

References available on request.

APPLYING FOR A JOB

WRITING YOUR PAPER-BASED CV

- Use clean, well-printed originals, using one easily legible font such as Arial or Helvetica.
- Use quality white paper of 90 or 100gsm. Avoid pretty pastel shades.
- Do not head the document 'Curriculum vitae': put your name and contact details at the top.
- Be brief – keep it to one or two pages. Omit irrelevant details such as your marital status/children/religion, reasons for leaving jobs and names and addresses of referees (unless the latter have been requested, in which case remember to brief your referees carefully about the potential job and warn them that someone might contact them). Also leave out qualifications that have become outdated or superseded by more recent qualifications or study you have undertaken, and keep to a minimum details of any jobs you did over 10 years ago.
- Beware of jargon and obscure abbreviations: write in plain English.
- Be specific – 'I have five years' experience in …' says far more than 'I have wide experience of …', as does 'I reduced inventory from £4.2m to £1.8m in a period of 12 months' compared with 'We made substantial savings by reducing our inventory'.
- Even if you can produce a decent letter it may be worth investing in getting someone to do your CV for you. If you need help with the content you could use a professional CV writer. Someone with professional secretarial skills could probably do a great deal to improve the presentation. Ask to see previous examples and make sure they give you a copy of the file for future updating and so that you can customise key strengths to produce a targeted CV to fit each job.
- Many software packages, including Microsoft Word, have CV

templates, but before you decide to use a template make sure that you are comfortable with the style, layout and content. It is your CV. And remember, if you are using the CV builder that came with your word processor it may end up looking just the same as those of all the other applicants using the same software. You can also find free CV writing software on the internet – just put 'CV software' into a search engine.

■ Proofread, proofread and proofread again. Start at the bottom of the page and read backwards. You may thimk there are no mistakes, but by reading backwards you see each word in isolation and can spot errors and mis-spellings. For example, did you spot 'thimk' in the last sentence or did you read what you thought was there?

■ If you have a name that could be interpreted as male or female, such as Jay or Frankie, add 'm' or 'f' after it in brackets (it puts recruiters off-balance when they phone candidates not knowing whether they will be talking to a man or a woman). If you think your name might cause confusion, you can also help recruiters if you explain. Name: John (given) Smith (family). And if you were named Rebecca at birth and are generally known as Becky, then put Becky on your CV. Remember, the CV is *your* marketing tool.

■ Leave a wide margin on the left-hand side: recruiters often like room to make notes.

■ CVs are often separated from letters of application. Use the header and footer facility to enter your name and contact details on each page, which will help if pages become separated. (It will also help an interviewer to remember your name when they are halfway through an interview and they have turned over the page.)

■ If you are applying for your first job or are returning to work after bringing up a family, help the recruiter to recognise your transferable skills. 'Chair of an outdoor pursuits society' and 'qualified mountain leader' implies leadership and someone trained to cope with adversity. 'Treasurer of the parish church council' implies financial skills and abilities to deal with contractors, etc., so spell it out for them.

THE LANGUAGE OF CVS

Striking a balance between being positive and sounding arrogant can be a real challenge.

Use active rather than passive words: 'I was responsible for managing a project team which installed a new intranet' says more than 'I was involved in installing a new intranet'. The first statement is far more powerful, while the second statement might mean no more than you plugged it in and switched it on. But beware: do not overdo it. Try reading your finished version to your partner or close friend. If you go a little pink you are probably spot-on (if your face turns bright red you have overdone it). If you are struggling for active words, here are some to help:

accomplished	co-ordinated	evaluated	instigated
achieved	corrected	expanded	interpreted
administered	counselled	experienced	introduced
adapted	created	flexible	invented
advised	decided	formed	investigated
arranged	demonstrated	formulated	led
assessed	dependable	friendly	literate
bought	developed	generated	maintained
built	devised	guided	managed
capable	doubled	handled	marketed
completed	economical	hard-working	methodical
cheerful	effective	implemented	modernised
combined	efficient	improved	monitored
communicated	employed	initiated	motivated
completed	engineered	inspired	negotiated
co-operated	established	increased	organised

originated	presented	recruited	succeeded
participated	produced	reliable	successful
patient	profitable	re-organised	supervised
performed	promoted	repaired	supported
planned	proposed	represented	tactful
polite	proved	responsible	teamwork
positive	punctual	revised	tested
practical	qualified	saved	trained
prepared	ran	simplified	versatile
problem-solving	recommended	solved	
processed	redesigned	specialised	

Do some research on yourself: complete the communication skills profile and the personality profiles at the end of this chapter. Look at your previous appraisals. What positive things do other people say about you? What do you consider to be your greatest strengths? Use all of these to build up a unique vocabulary which describes you, and use this in your CV.

CV CHECKLIST

Items that *should* be included are in **bold**, while those that *could* be included are in *italics*. Ultimately, however, it is your CV and you are totally in control of what you include.

- **Name, address, email address and telephone number(s),** with best daytime contact number first
- *Nationality*
- *Date of birth/age* (see advice on pages 76–7)
- **School, college/university attended** (normally from age of 11 onwards)
- **Qualifications:** put these at the front if you have a first-class honours degree, PhD or MBA. You may wish to leave your qualifications to the end if your business achievements outshine your academic ones. While a recent graduate

looking for a first job would state GCSEs indicating level, subjects and pass grade, along with degree subjects taken and class of degree, a 51-year-old divisional director need only say something along the lines of '6 O-levels, 3 A-levels, BSc 2(i) Chemistry'
- *Language proficiency*
- *Willingness to relocate*, especially if you live beyond commuting distance (omit if you are not)
- *Career history (for chronological CVs)*: current/last job first, then work backwards through your career, allocating most space to recent job(s) with brief mentions of your early career. Give a one- or two-sentence summary of the company products/services and annual turnover, then summarise your responsibilities and achievements against each job. Reduce the information as you go back, e.g. five achievements for your current/most recent job, three from a job you had two years ago, but only one from a job you had 15 years ago
- *Current/last salary and benefits package*, e.g. company car. Be brief. (Opinions differ on whether salary should be included: you may wish to keep your cards close to your chest and risk missing an opportunity because the recruiter thinks you might be too expensive)
- *Career aims*
- *Personal strengths*: a four- or five-sentence summary of who you are and what you have to offer (make every word count)
- *Leisure activities*: be realistic and do not exaggerate your leisure skills (a one-week skiing holiday five years ago does not qualify you as a skier). Include a variety to show that you have broad interests, but not too many or the recruiter may wonder how you ever find time for work. Three to four interests will be adequate
- *Professional achievements*, e.g. titles of research papers or articles you have had published (but do not attach the papers)

- *Memberships of professional institutions* and whether by examination or election
- *Names of referees:* omit unless you are applying for a job in the public sector
- *Driving licence (if relevant):* note that 'clean' and 'current' do not mean the same
- *Evidence of continuing professional development (CPD):* see Appendix II.

Target your CV to the job: read the job description thoroughly and see if you need to expand on anything or leave anything out so that you match the requirements.

Use similar expressions in your CV to those the recruiter has used in the job advert/job description. If you think that you are meticulous and the employer wants someone who is thorough, say that you are thorough. In the era of word-processing and electronic communication there is no excuse for not adapting your CV to fit the job.

PAPER APPLICATION FORMS

Organisations use application forms, either online or paper, for two main reasons:

1 to collect 'standard information' on all candidates, so that the person doing the initial screening can easily compare candidates against each other and against the job;
2 to oblige candidates to provide certain important information: for example, while a CV may simply state 'full driving licence', an application form might say, 'Give details of any driving licence endorsements', which might reveal a number of penalty points and what violations gave rise to them.

From one point of view, an application form is a chore, but more positively it could be regarded as a perfectly targeted CV. When you complete one:

- read the form before writing anything
- make a copy of the blank form to use for drafting your answers
- complete the form as requested (black ink does not mean blue ink, no matter how dark)
- if you need to use extra pages, write your name and job applied for, plus the reference, at the top of each page
- match your application to the job: review the job advertisement and any other relevant information you have, such as the full job description, background on the organisation, etc.
- answer all of the questions
- explain any gaps in your career
- maximise the 'Other information' opportunity by making a positive statement about you
- use feature and benefit statements to relate your past experience to the skills and qualities they are
- do not include any negatives about yourself – this is not the place to be self-effacing
- telephone referees before putting them on the application
- proofread, proofread, proofread – and get someone else to do it as well
- photocopy the completed form – so that you know what you have said when you are invited for interview
- use first-class post or recorded delivery, or, for a top job, use a courier service.

ONLINE APPLICATION FORMS

Take your time with online forms and be as thorough as you would if you were writing by hand.

Print off the questions and compose your replies on your computer, so that you can copy and paste them into the form.

Many applications have a word count limit for different sections to force the applicant to be concise. Use the word count facility to keep checking, and edit ruthlessly. Remember that when you apply online the application will take you through a number of stages, and will also ask you a number of times to check and then to confirm before you click 'submit' – so you can have a dry run without actually applying.

Read the advertisement and try to second-guess any special requirements or words that the recruiter will be looking for. Include 'keywords' for your skills and experience. When you are completely satisfied that you have got it right, and have checked your spellings for the last time, go back online and copy and paste your text into the application form. Make a final check and 'submit application'. You will probably get an almost instant email acknowledgement – which is a function of the software, not an indication that someone is already reading what you sent.

STRETCHING THE TRUTH WHEN APPLYING FOR JOBS

Thinking of stretching the truth or even including blatant lies in your CV? You might just get away with it – but there is a chance that you will not. Even if you do manage to start a new job it is likely that the truth will catch up with you.

A CV is designed to sell you to your prospective employer, but it is not a place for lying. Lies or deliberate distortions could get you a job, but just as quickly you could find yourself out on the street.

According to a 2007 survey by the Chartered Institute of Personnel and Development of over 700 UK employers, a quarter of employers in the UK had withdrawn at least one job offer in the previous 12 months after discovering someone had lied or misrepresented something on their application. And almost as many (23 per cent) had dismissed someone who had started to work for them for the same offence.

Employers do make checks, by taking up references from previous employers; also, an increasing number of jobs involve a Criminal Record Bureau (CRB) check.

REHABILITATION OF OFFENDERS ACT 1974

If you committed a criminal offence in the past and were sentenced, you may be able to leave out of your CV any mention of the fact that you were in prison if the offence has become 'spent'.

The Rehabilitation of Offenders Act 1974 allows some criminal convictions to become 'spent', or ignored, after a 'rehabilitation period'.

Your rehabilitation period is set from the date of your conviction. After this, with certain exceptions, you are not normally obliged to mention your conviction when applying for a job.

The Act is more likely to help you if you have few and/or minor convictions (because of the way further convictions extend the rehabilitation period). If you have many convictions, especially if they are serious, you may not benefit from the Act at all unless the last convictions are very old.

The length of the rehabilitation period depends on the sentence, not the offence committed. And for a custodial sentence, the length of time you served is not taken into consideration. The rehabilitation period is decided by the original sentence. Custodial sentences of more than 2¹/₂ years can never become spent.

For more information visit the websites mentioned in chapter 7.

PERSONALITY AND BEHAVIOURAL EVALUATIONS

Effective communication with others is a key skill for helping you to achieve your career and life goals. This section introduces you to a process which will give you a deeper understanding of your communication and working style. Completing and analysing the questionnaire on the following pages will help you to understand how to get along better with other people; it will also give you some insight into the kind of work to which you might be best suited.

When you are being interviewed you will be asked questions which dig deep into the kind of person that you are. By completing the questionnaire you will be far better equipped to handle the interview questions. Finally, the questionnaire will help you enormously in putting your CV and applications together as the results will give you a vocabulary for describing your personal qualities and skills.

You do not need to be told that people's personalities vary enormously. Some people are the life and soul of the party, dress flamboyantly and speak fast in loud voices; get two of them together and there is almost a competition to see who can burst the other's eardrums first. If you approach one of these people in a mild-mannered, matter-of-fact way you are unlikely to make an impression.

Other people like to conduct business very formally, and are so focused on getting to the point that they can seem positively abrupt. If you take up meeting time with convivial questions about family, hobbies and what they did during the weekend you will probably have burned up 80 per cent of the time they have allocated for the meeting.

It is often said that if you want to understand other people and get along with them better, the best starting point is to understand yourself.

The communication style inventory on the following pages will help you to understand your own preferred communication style.

Be honest and realistic when completing your answers. Do not complete the inventory as you think you should act, or as you would like to act, but how you believe you *do* actually act in work situations. Give each question a certain amount of thought. There is no time limit and there are no trick questions. Once you have completed the inventory you will be able to analyse your results and read about your preferred communication style.

COMMUNICATION STYLE INVENTORY

This inventory (CSI–SADI) contains 28 pairs of statements that relate to the way people behave in work situations. For each pair of statements you have five points to distribute between the two alternatives (A and B). Base your answers on your knowledge of your behaviour. Your scores must be whole numbers – not fractions.

How to score your answers. If …

A is very characteristic of me. B is very uncharacteristic.

A = 5 and B = 0

A is fairly characteristic of me. B is fairly uncharacteristic.

A = 4 and B = 1

A is more characteristic of me than B. A = 3 and B = 2

B is more characteristic of me than A. B = 3 and A = 2

B is fairly characteristic of me. A is fairly uncharacteristic.

B = 4 and A = 1

B is very characteristic of me. A is very uncharacteristic.

B = 5 and A = 0

Remember, the numbers you assign to each pair of statements must add up to 5.

Example: **When I think about my own decision-making style:**
A is fairly characteristic of me. B is fairly uncharacteristic.
So I would mark my responses as follows:

17A _4_ am fast-paced in my decision-making

17B _1_ take time to reach well thought-out decisions

When thinking about my behaviour with other people at work, I:

1A ___ prefer an informal and relaxed work environment

1B ___ prefer a formal and businesslike work environment

2A ___ am slow and deliberate in my actions

2B ___ am fast and spontaneous in my actions

3A ___ am adaptable in my approach to people and situations

3B ___ am predictable in my approach to people and situations

4A ___ am disciplined and structured about the way other people use my time

4B ___ am flexible, about the way other people use my time

5A ___ express my opinions freely in groups, without being asked

5B ___ tend to contribute in groups, when invited to do so

6A ___ am usually willing to negotiate the outcome of situations

6B ___ am usually reluctant to negotiate the outcome of situations

7A ___ focus on the feelings and opinions of others during discussions

7B ___ focus on the facts and business issues during discussions

8A ___ respond to conflict situations slowly and indirectly

8B ___ respond to conflict situations quickly and directly

9A ___ am usually willing to change my opinions and ideas

9B ___ am not usually willing to change my opinions and ideas

10A ___ keep my personal feelings and thoughts private

10B ___ discuss my feelings freely with others

11A ___ take the initiative to introduce myself in social situations

11B ___ tend to wait for others to introduce themselves to me in social situations

12A ___ am flexible in my approach to dealing with people and situations

12B ___ am predictable in my approach to dealing with people and situations

13A ___ prefer to work in a group with others

13B ___ prefer to work on my own

14A ___ am cautious and predictable in my approach to risk and change

14B ___ am dynamic and unpredictable in my approach to risk and change

15A ___ quickly adapt to new systems and working practices

15B ___ like to take my time to adapt to new systems and working practices

16A ___ prefer to focus primarily on business ideas and results

16B ___ prefer to focus primarily on people and their feelings

17A ___ am fast-paced in my decision-making

17B ___ take time to reach well thought-out decisions

18A ___ like to cope with many different situations at the same time

18B ___ prefer to handle one thing at a time

19A ___ tend to get to know many people personally

19B ___ tend to get to know only a few people personally

20A___ tend to keep my opinions to myself, and prefer to offer them when asked

20B ___ state my opinions freely, without being asked

21A___ tend to make my decisions based on facts or evidence

21B ___ tend to make my decisions based on feelings or opinions

22A ___ like to actively seek out new experiences and situations

22B ___ tend to choose known or familiar situations and relationships

23A___ am an intuitive decision-maker

23B ___ am a rational decision-maker

24A___ am non-confrontational, and comfortable with a slow pace

24B ___ am direct with others, and can be impatient when things move slowly

25A___ share my personal feelings and emotions in conversations

25B ___ control my personal feelings and emotions in conversation

26A___ tend to dominate conversation in group discussions

26B ___ tend to make infrequent well-thought-out inputs in group discussions

27A___ am more interested in people's opinions than facts

27B ___ am more interested in facts than people's opinions

28A___ tend to move at a controlled pace

28B ___ tend to move at a fast pace

(CSI–SADI and the four circle model © Delta-Management)

Scoring When you have completed the inventory and checked to make sure that the score for each pair of questions adds up to five, transfer your scores to the table overleaf.

Please take care when transferring your scores as the A–B order changes in some of the questions.

E	R	S	L	SAH + (These are positive + numbers)	SAL – (These are negative – numbers)
1A	1B	2B	2A	3A +	3B –
4B	4A	5A	5B	6A +	6B –
7A	7B	8B	8A	9A +	9B –
10B	10A	11A	11B	12A +	12B –
13A	13B	14B	14A	15A +	15B –
16B	16A	17A	17B	18A +	18B –
19A	19B	20B	20A		
21B	21A	22A	22B		
23A	23B	24B	24A		
25A	25B	26A	26B		
27A	27B	28B	28A		
E Total	R Total	S Total	L Total	SAH Total +	SAL Total –

Compare the **E** and **R** scores. Which is higher? Write the higher score in the space below and circle the corresponding letter:

_____   E   R

Compare the **S** and **L** scores. Which is higher? Write the higher score in the space below and circle the corresponding letter:

_____   S   L

Style adaptability score: _____

To calculate this combine your SAH and SAL scores to give you a number ranging from (plus) +30 to (minus) –30. SAH are positive numbers, SAL are negative (minus) numbers.

YOUR COMMUNICATION STYLE

By completing the above communication style inventory you have given an indication of your preferred way of communicating with others.

By the time we reach our mid- to late twenties, most people have become comfortable with a particular style. Understanding your own style and the styles of others can help to make meetings with other people more productive. The main objective of understanding communication style is to help you to develop style adaptability in dealing with others.

Calculating your CSI–SADI scores will show your preferred communication style. This should help you to understand how you might 'come across' to others, and will help you to plan how you can deal more effectively with other people. If you are:

E and L your style is	**S**upporter
L and R your style is	**A**nalyst
R and S your style is	**D**irector
E and S your style is	**I**nstigator

There is no 'best' style. And as you read about the four styles, you will probably say, 'I can be all of these'. You probably can. The fact is that we all have our own preferred style. All of us have the potential ability to adopt different styles at various times. What you have identified by completing the inventory is your 'comfort zone'.

As you can see from the four-circle diagram overleaf, there are four communication-style comfort zones and they all overlap in the middle. At times we can adopt any of the communication styles, but most of the time we prefer to stick to our comfort zone. You will probably find that if you move from your comfort zone, it is easier to move to the circles on either side of your comfort zone. It is usually most difficult to move to the circle directly opposite yours, because the communication style which is the direct opposite of yours is farthest from your comfort zone.

THE FOUR CSI–SADI COMMUNICATION STYLES

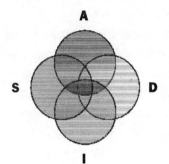

Supporter
Analyst
Director
Instigator

Understanding your CSI–SADI communication style can help you relate to other
people in a better way. By knowing your
own style, and knowing how to recognise
the style of others, you can improve communication.

Of course, there are two sides to every coin: for example, the
self-confident 'director' may be interpreted as an insensitive steamroller by other people and the accurate 'analyst' may be seen as
pedantic and nitpicking. The helpful 'supporter' could be considered
weak and wishy-washy while the inspiring 'instigator' may be seen as
insincere and shallow. As you read more about your preferred style
on the following pages, try to think about how other people might
interpret your behaviour.

Your communication style can also give you some clues on your
preferred working environment, and maybe some ideas on the kind
of work you may prefer.

Supporter

Supporters are 'naturals' when it comes to relating to others. You are: co-operative, a natural team player, slow-paced,
trusting, quiet, supportive, friendly, a good listener, non-
confrontational, sensitive, patient, understanding, generous, helpful,
personable and unassuming. People see your communication style as:
quiet, supportive and helpful, accommodating, loyal and able to empathise.
You probably prefer a working environment where:
You are allowed or encouraged to think over ideas before implement-
ing them. You are able to stand back from events and listen and watch
before making decisions. You are allowed to think before acting or

commenting. You can carry out research and investigate, assemble information and probe to get to the bottom of things. You are asked to produce carefully considered analyses and reports. You can reach a decision in your own time without pressure and tight deadlines. You have the opportunity for regular contact with a variety of people.

You probably will not enjoy working where:
You are forced to be high-profile and act as leader/chairman/presenter. You are involved in situations that require action without planning. You are pitched into doing something without warning, like producing an instant reaction or an instant idea. You are given insufficient data on which to base a conclusion. You are given instructions of how things should be done, without involving others. You are worried by time pressures, or rushed from one task to another. You have to take short cuts or do a superficial job.

Questions to ask yourself:
Will I be given adequate time to consider, assimilate and prepare my work? Will there be opportunities and facilities to organise my work? Will there be opportunities to work with a wide variety of other people and incorporate their ideas into my work? Will I be under pressure to work to tight deadlines, which may result in sloppy work?

Typical job roles: admin assistant, bartender, coach, counsellor, diplomat, general practitioner, mediator, minister, missionary, nurse, psychologist, PR executive, receptionist, salesperson, social worker, teacher.

The strengths you will bring to the job: you facilitate team working and co-operation, diffuse conflict, create a friendly impression with people; you create a relaxed and unruffled atmosphere; you are loyal.

Analyst

Analysts like to consider all of the options and move slowly, but precisely. You are: logical, a natural planner, quality focused, analytical, organised, focused, exact, a perfectionist, structured, a good listener, independent, controlled, cool, non-aggressive, disciplined, deliberate and businesslike. People see your communication style as: structured and organised; quiet and unassuming; factual and logical; practical and controlled; cautious and conscientious.

You probably prefer a working environment where:

You work within a system. You can methodically explore the associations and interrelationships between ideas, events and situations. You have the chance to question and probe the basic methodology, assumptions or logic, like checking a report for inconsistencies. You are working with high-calibre people, who ask searching questions which intellectually stretch you. You are in structured situations with a clear purpose. You are required to understand and participate in complex situations.

You probably will not enjoy working where:

You have to do things without a context or apparent purpose, like doing things just for the fun of it. You have to work in situations that focus on emotions and feelings. You are involved in unstructured work where there is a lot of ambiguity and uncertainty. You have to make decisions without guidelines or policies. You find the work shallow or gimmicky and without real purpose. You have to work with people of a lower intellectual calibre.

Questions to ask yourself:

Will there be lots of opportunities to question my work? Is the work clear, structured and purposeful? Will I work on complex ideas and concepts that are likely to stretch me? Are the working systems tested, sound and valid?

Typical job roles: accountant, building inspector, business analyst, city planner, computer programmer, data processor, efficiency expert, engineer, investigator, IT/technical salesperson, military strategist, museum curator, proofreader, quality control inspector, researcher, secretary, administrator, solicitor, surgeon, statistician.

The strengths you will bring to the job: your attention to detail and production of top-quality work; logical and analytical work methods; the ability to do tedious work, for long periods, alone.

Director

Directors prefer to be in control of situations. You are: businesslike, a natural leader, goal-centred, fast-paced, task-oriented, assertive, decisive, confident, determined, competitive, independent, straightforward, direct, an achiever, challenging, correct, you take the initiative, confront, are quick, opportunistic and forceful. People see your communication style as: in-charge, efficient, direct, quick and controlled.

You probably prefer a working environment where:
You are given autonomy in decision-making. You are in charge. You have the chance to try out and practise things, and get feedback from someone whom you respect because of their expertise. You respect your boss as an expert. You can implement your ideas quickly. You work on practical issues like drawing up action plans, suggesting short cuts and giving tips. You learn techniques for doing things with obvious practical advantages like how to do a job more quickly, how to make a good first impression, or how to deal with awkward people.

You probably will not enjoy working where:
You find the work irrelevant, esoteric or unrelated to an immediate need. You cannot see the results of your efforts. You cannot see immediate relevance or practical benefits. You feel colleagues are out of touch with reality, pompous, or live in ivory towers. There is no practice or clear guidelines on how to do it. People go round in circles without getting anywhere. There are lots of politics and protocols. You cannot see a relationship between your work and the real world.

Questions to ask yourself:
Will I be given a free rein to do things my way? Will there be lots of practical help and resources? Does the job address real issues? Will I have a boss who knows how to/can do it? Will I be stretched?

Typical job roles: business coach, business manager, conductor, director, foreman, head waiter, military officer, negotiator, running own business, personnel manager, pilot, police officer, chief executive, project leader, sales manager, security guard, shop steward, supervisor.

The strengths you will bring to the job: you can take charge and set goals, can finish a lot of jobs quickly and work to tight deadlines; you take control and do not shy away from conflict.

Instigator

Instigators like to get things going and then move on. You are: inspiring, a natural risk-taker, ideas-driven, creative, innovative, flexible, visionary, spontaneous, enthusiastic, free-spirited, energising, emotional, friendly, sociable, intuitive, an initiator, political, excitable and a doer. People see your communication style as: comforting and fun, people-centred, ambitious and competitive; inspiring and exciting; motivating.

You probably prefer a working environment where:

There are new experiences, problems and opportunities. You can immerse yourself in short projects with tight deadlines. The environment is exciting and things change regularly with a range of diverse activities to tackle. You have a good deal of the limelight/high visibility, as in chairing meetings, leading discussions and giving presentations. You are allowed to generate ideas without constraints of policy or structure. You are thrown in at the deep end with difficult problems. You are involved with other people brainstorming ideas and solving problems, as part of a team. You feel you are free to 'have a go', to try new ideas and ways of doing things.

You probably will not enjoy working where:

You have a passive role, with no involvement in decision-making. You are required to assimilate, analyse and interpret lots of data. You have to work alone most of the time. You have to work on theoretical concepts. You have to repeat the same activity over and over again. You have precise instructions, policies and procedures to follow with little room for your interpretation. You are required to be pedantic and attend to lots of detail.

Questions to ask yourself:

Will I learn something new in the job that I did not know or could not do before? Will there be a wide variety of different activities? Will it be OK to have a go, let my hair down, make mistakes and have some fun? Will I work on tough problems and challenges? Will I get a chance to demonstrate my success?

Typical job roles: activities leader, advertising account executive, architect, artist, builder, business strategist, chief executive, estate agent, events director, explorer, head-hunter, landscaper, performer, presenter, project director, property developer, PR executive, tour guide, writer.

The strengths you will bring to the job: your creative ideas and talents; versatility and an ability to win people over; innovative and unconventional thinking; free-spirited risk-taking; an ability to act quickly.

THE FOUR CSI–SADI COMMUNICATION STYLES

SUPPORTER

- Needs co-operation, personal security and acceptance
- Uncomfortable with and will avoid conflict
- Values personal relationships, helping others and being liked
- May sacrifice their own desires to win approval from others
- Prefers to work with other people in a team effort, rather than individually
- Has an unhurried reaction time and prefers the status quo
- Friendly, supportive, respectful, willing, dependable and agreeable
- People-oriented
- Uses opinions and stories rather than facts and data
- Speaks slowly and softly
- Leans back while talking and does not make direct eye contact
- Has an informal posture and an animated expression
- Perceived by others as conforming, unsure, pliable, dependent and awkward
- Homely office space – family photographs, plants etc.

ANALYST

- Concerned with being organised, having all the facts and being careful before taking action
- Precise, orderly and

methodical and conforms to standard operating procedures, organisational rules and established ways of doing things

ANALYST CONTINUED

○ Needs to be accurate and to be right

○ Has a slow reaction time and works slowly and carefully

○ Perceived as serious, industrious, persistent and exacting

○ Uses facts and data

○ Tends to speak slowly and want lots of information

○ Leans back and uses hands infrequently

○ Task-oriented

○ Does not make direct eye contact

○ Controls facial expressions

○ Can be perceived as stuffy, indecisive, critical, picky and moralistic

○ Comfortable in positions in which they can check facts and figures and be sure they are right

○ Neat/well organised office

INSTIGATOR

○ Enjoys involvement, excitement and action

○ Social, stimulating and enthusiastic and good at involving and motivating others

○ Ideas- and future-orientated

○ Has little concern for routine

○ Has a quick reaction time

○ Needs to be accepted by others

○ Tends to be spontaneous, outgoing and energetic

○ Focused on people rather than tasks

○ Uses opinions and stories rather than facts and data

○ Speaks and acts quickly; varies vocal inflection

○ Leans forward, points and makes direct eye contact

○ Uses hands when talking

○ Has a relaxed bodily posture and an animated expression

○ Feelings often show in face

○ Perceived as excitable, impulsive, undisciplined, dramatic, manipulative, ambitious, overly reactive and egotistical

○ Disorganised office: may contain leisure equipment like golf clubs or tennis racquets

DIRECTOR

- Action and goal-oriented
- Needs to see results
- Has a quick reaction time and is decisive, independent, disciplined, practical and efficient
- Uses facts and data
- Speaks and acts quickly
- Leans forward and points and makes direct eye contact
- Rigid body posture
- Controlled facial expressions
- Does not want to waste time on personal talk or preliminaries
- Can be perceived as dominating or harsh and severe in pursuit of a goal
- Comfortable in positions of power and control
- Businesslike office with certificates and commendations on the wall

STYLE ADAPTABILITY

There is no 'best' style. The key to using this process is style adaptability. About a quarter of the population have a similar 'style' to yours and so you will probably find that you are comfortable with them.

You have probably noticed that some people are naturally very adaptable and are able to accommodate easily to the needs of other people. Others are less skilled and are often seen as inflexible or maybe even downright difficult. **By developing your adaptability skills, you will be able get on with more people.**

Why is this so important? Because as a private individual you have complete freedom of choice in terms of whom you socialise with, whom you like, and whom you do not like. But to be successful at work you must have the skills to get along with all kinds of different people. If you know what makes you tick, and have an insight into what makes your subordinates, your colleagues and your managers tick, you have made a pretty good start on the journey.

The people to whom you probably find it most difficult to relate naturally are your 'opposites'. Study the characteristics of your opposite style.

Think about how you can adapt your behaviour, i.e. improve your style adaptability, next time you meet someone from your 'opposite style'. For example, 'analysts' may need to warm up when dealing with 'instigators' and be prepared to be interviewed over a pie and a pint or in the gym – just because the surroundings are informal does not make the meeting less important. 'Instigators' need to be specific and factual in their contacts with 'analysts'; be precise about what you say and give them time to assimilate it, and make decisions. 'Supporters' need to get to the point when dealing with 'directors' – chitchat about family and hobbies would be wasted on 'directors'. Similarly, 'directors' need to slow things down and indulge in friendly conversation when meeting with 'supporters', in order to develop a trusting relationship.

Now transfer your style adaptability score from the inventory on to the scale that follows: how did you score?

+30	+25	+20	+15	+10	+5	–5	–10	–15	–20	–25	–30
High					0						Low

ACQUIRING THE SKILL TO ADAPT YOUR STYLE

Style adaptability is a skill which can be learned and developed. Some people are 'naturally' more adaptable than others. By being more adaptable you will make other people feel more comfortable about being in your company. Your score is not fixed: you can develop your style adaptability, and the more you adapt, the easier it becomes to get on with different people. How did you score?

Low score (0 to –30)

This may mean that you are reluctant to 'bend' to the needs of others – your approach is 'Take me as I am', or 'What you see is what you get'. You like to do things for your own reasons, rather than other people's. You hide behind your job title and use your 'position power' to get things done, rather than the 'personal power' of your influencing skills. You may be predictable and have a low sensitivity to differences between people, which causes you to act in a predictable way. Your presence may make other people uncomfortable.

High score (+20 to +30)

This may mean that you are very willing to adapt to meet the needs of other people. You easily see other people's reasons for doing things. You do not hide behind your job title, but use the 'personal power' of your influencing skills, rather than the power of your position. You can be unpredictable. You spend more time thinking about what makes other people happy than what makes you happy.

Of course, life is not black or white and the above descriptions describe the two absolute ends of the adaptability scale. Unless you scored +30, think about this. Look back at your answers to the inventory. Ask yourself the question: 'What can I do to improve my style adaptability?'

Remember, style adaptability is a skill. You can learn it and build on it. Being aware of your preferred style and understanding your style adaptability can help you to develop better relationships.

PERSONALITY EVALUATIONS

Many organisations use personality questionnaires as part of their selection process. You will find it really useful to have an insight into your own personality prior to making your application. The world's most widely used personality questionnaire is called the Myers-Briggs Type Inventory, or MBTI for short.

You can only administer the MBTI if you have been specially trained and so access to the MBTI is restricted. You can however take an online version of the MBTI which was developed a number of years ago. This is known as the Keirsey Temperament Sorter and started life in the book *Please Understand Me*, by David Keirsey PhD. The test claims to be the number 1 online personality assessment, and is well worth doing. To take the Keirsey Temperament Sorter you will need to register on the site www.keirsey.com.

Beware of other online personality sites. Put the expression 'personality test' into a search engine and it will come up with hundreds of sites, but it is difficult to know how safe it is to give out personal information to those who run them – and you cannot know how valid or otherwise their results will be. ■

> 'Take stock of what you want in your job, keep at it, maybe go freelance or take an interim management post, if you're a professional, to keep yourself and your skills current – and network like crazy. Cultivate relationships with recruiters, make sure your CV sells you well, set up email alerts on the appropriate job boards, and attend recruitment events. Think about running your own business. Above all, have faith in yourself.' *(marketing professional, female, 48, who found it very difficult to get a full-time job after being made redundant but has successfully carved out a new career path)*

4

WINNING IN THE SELECTION PROCESS

WINNING IN THE SELECTION PROCESS

'Most employers are surprisingly positive about their older workers, though less so about recruiting older workers – "better the devil you know" than the one you don't (whatever their age).' *(Professor Stephen McNair, Director, Centre for Research into the Older Workforce, NIACE)*

Employers use numerous different ways of selecting candidates, from online screening processes through to assessment centres. According to research carried out by the Chartered Institute of Personnel and Development, the most popular selection method continues to be the 1:1 or 1:2 interview, so this chapter will look at how you can convince the interviewer that you are the best person for the job. It will also look at other selection methods, such as panel interviews, assessment centres and how to give a presentation.

Not 'selling' yourself at interview is where many older candidates fail in the selection process, and so this section includes a large number of tips on how to handle yourself in the interview process. If you have not attended a job interview for a good number of years you will probably find that things have changed a lot. Recruiters are now trying to be smarter in their selection, and the style of questioning which some of them use will be different from what you have experienced in the past.

RECRUITMENT INTERVIEWS

The day of reckoning approaches. You have trawled the newspapers and the internet to find the job you want. You followed the application procedure meticulously and submitted a well-crafted letter of application and CV. Today you opened your email folder and there it is – you have received an invitation to an interview. What a mixed emotion that can be – possibly a feeling of elation at the prospect of being nearer to the finishing line tempered by an absolute dread of the event itself.

Most people approach the prospect of a job interview with some degree of apprehension, and this may be compounded if you have not had a job interview for a long time. But try not to let that affect your performance (performance? Yes, the interview *is* a performance). Most managers do not normally sit in meeting rooms all day interviewing candidates. And given the choice, most candidates would rather be getting on with the job than being interviewed. But the reality is that both have to go through the interview process… and both are looking forward to a positive outcome.

> 'Job seekers who have been absent from the labour market for a while often lack confidence in their ability, and undersell their achievements. Lack of awareness from job seekers on what employers want (good communication skills, reliability, able to get on with a job and work without constant supervision etc.) mean they do not focus on this at interview and age is then used (by the individual, not the employer) as the reason for de-selection rather than their inability to "crack" the interview/selection process.' *(Karol Doveston, NEPL (Able to Work Project), Jobcentre Plus Liaison Manager)*

MAKING THE INTERVIEWER'S JOB EASIER

If you think about it, there is a good chance that you are older than the person who will be interviewing you. You might have better qualifications, and you might even have a better track record of success. But when push comes to shove, they have a job and you want one.

In the interview, do what you can to sell yourself as someone who is confident and competent, but not cocky and condescending. Arrogance, oddly enough, is one of the biggest 'own goals' scored by senior candidates.

The interviewer might have had little or no training or experience and may be daunted by the interview process, as you are. Help the interviewer by making a clear and succinct case for why you are the best candidate.

THE POWER OF SELF-BELIEF

Believe in yourself and it will be easier to convince the interviewer to believe in you.

Research for this book revealed that many older candidates 'shoot themselves in the foot' during interviews, by making self-effacing remarks stemming from low self-esteem.

The recruitment interview is not a counselling session or a careers advice session: it is for real. You really *must* enter the interview feeling that you want the job and that you can do the job. Cast aside any self-doubt and focus on who you are (positive attitude) and what you can do (skills, and what you know – i.e. knowledge).

RESEARCH AND PREPARATION

The most important factor for a candidate in an interview is preparation. It is vital to know about the organisation, the position and how you match up to the job. Do not forget that the employer has asked to meet you because, based on your application and CV, they think you are capable of doing the job. Their time is precious and they will be hoping, just like you, that you can fill the vacancy. Your CV and letter of application have done their work and now it is time for you to convince the interviewer that you are the right person for the job.

Prepare carefully and practise for your interview. You can do this by answering the questions with a friend.

Decide on an acceptable financial package – but at the interview leave it to the interviewer to raise the issue of money.

Knowing about the organisation will increase your confidence and that, in turn, will improve your chances. Do not rely on charm and wit – there is too much at stake. Interviewers like well prepared candidates who show a genuine interest in joining their organisation.

Find out everything you can about the job, the organisation and its products or services. Visit the organisation's website and use Google or another search engine to help you to find out more. Get a copy of the annual report: if it is a public limited company (plc), voluntary sector or public sector organisation, an annual report must be provided on request (often, you can access annual reports via the organisation's website). Phone the PR, HR or communications department, or go to the premises in person. Read product literature on the organisation's leading products, goods or services. Research what type of organisation it is – public, private, family-owned, parent company, voluntary/charity sector, etc. – and about its performance compared with its competitors'.

The internet is of course key to carrying out this research, and in today's information-rich environment you may as well not bother turning up for interview if you have not done some basic online delving.

As obvious as all of this might sound, candidates do still attend interviews knowing little or nothing about their potential employer. Neglecting to put in a modicum of effort on this front is likely to ensure you are not shortlisted.

After you have done your research, you need to understand and assimilate it. What does it tell you about the organisation's mission, its corporate culture, its approach to those it serves (its clients, customers, service users, beneficiaries or whatever)? There is no point simply going to the interview with a sheaf of printouts. The interviewer will want to know that you have read and absorbed the information, that you like what you have found out and want to be part of it.

Now you need to think about going the extra mile so that you can distinguish yourself from the rest of the pack.

Check that you are up to date with developments in your field – scan the trade journals and the internet. What are the four or five latest innovations/initiatives/developments/trends – and what are your opinions of them? Read the local newspaper and national newspaper, and scan any articles that might be directly related to the organisation or the field in which it operates. Make a mental note of the main news stories of the day and formulate a view/opinion.

If you can, talk to people who use the organisation's products or services.

A man with no experience of selling surgical implants (a somewhat specialised field) applied for a job selling replacement heart valves. Before the interview, he went to the cardiac department of a large London teaching hospital and spoke to some of the surgical team about their use of replacement heart valves. He was invited to spend a day in an operating theatre seeing the products in use. All he did was ask – and having gained this insight into the product and its function, he got the job.

Another job seeker, considering a career change, was wondering whether to re-train as a plumber. He contacted a local firm of plumbers who let him work alongside one of their plumbers for a couple of days as an unpaid helper. When he applied for a training course at the local college he got straight on to the course, because he knew what he was letting himself in for. He had also made an impression on the plumbing firm and was asked to get in contact again when he qualified.

PRE-INTERVIEW PRACTICALITIES

Find out who will be interviewing you (including their job titles) and think about what they might be looking for. This is particularly important if you are applying for a promotion or you already know the organisation well.

Make sure you know the time, date and location of the interview, how to get to the interview and how long it will take you to make the journey.

If it is at all practical, do a dummy run.

Arrive early so that you can prepare yourself mentally and relax. Lord Nelson is reputed to have said, 'I owe my success in life to always being 15 minutes before my time.' The principle is sound. However, try not to arrive more than 15 minutes before the interview – wait

outside rather than having yourself announced too early. Some people could see arriving much too early as poor time management. They
may also be embarrassed to keep you waiting for a long time.

Plan your journey. There is virtually no excuse for being late for
an interview. Allow extra time for the vagaries of public transport,
rush-hour traffic, road works and finding a parking space. Allow for
delays. If for any reason you are delayed and you know you are going
to be late, let the organisation or agency know you have a problem.
Railway station and motorway closures and other crises can happen.
Recruiters live in the real world and will usually be flexible in such
circumstances. Make sure you have the recruiter's phone number
before you set out for the interview.

Dress smartly for the interview in well-pressed, comfortable
clothes appropriate to the job/organisation.

Try on what you are going to wear in advance, to make sure you
are happy with the look and also to make sure that the clothes fit.
As general rule, do not wear your outfit for the first time on this occasion, because if it rubs or chafes or is too tight or too loose it will
affect your self-confidence. Try to match the look and culture of the
organisation and then dress a notch or two above average.

If possible, prior to the interview, discreetly visit the premises and
watch the employees as they enter and leave the building to see what
they are wearing. If in doubt, always dress 'up' rather than down. As
a general rule of thumb you cannot go far wrong in a smart, dark-
coloured suit.

If your hair needs a trim, schedule that for shortly before the
interview. Do what you can to make yourself feel good – if you feel
good inside, you will present yourself well on the outside.

Travel light, with only one bag or briefcase.

ARRIVING FOR THE INTERVIEW

When you arrive, have a good look around. Could you work in these
conditions? Do people seem comfortable talking to each other? What

is your impression of the culture? Is it formal or informal, and can you see yourself fitting in?

When you speak to receptionists and PAs, remember that they may be asked for their comments. If you are given an 'informal' tour of the site or offices before the interview, the person who acts as guide is also likely to be asked for their impressions.

Leave your raincoat and umbrella in reception, so that you walk into the interview room unencumbered by clutter, and switch off your mobile phone.

Then comes the moment you have been waiting for, when you are called into the room.

Now is your opportunity to convince the interviewers that *you* are the one they should select.

During the interview you need to convince the interviewer that:

- you can do the job competently (perhaps not immediately, but definitely after induction and training)
- you will be an asset to the organisation
- you are the best candidate.

In order to do this, you need to communicate effectively.

COMMUNICATION SKILLS

Most of us are poor listeners.

'Sorry, did you say something?'

Yes – most of us are poor listeners. We are often so concerned with what we are going to ask or say next that we ignore or miss a lot of what the other person says. Improving your active listening skills *will* improve your chances in interviews.

Many of the people who read this book will have received some guidelines, training or coaching in 'talking to groups' at some time in their career. You have certainly been taught how to read and write. But the likelihood is that you have never been trained in listening skills

— even though it is the communication skill that you use more than any other. Look at the table below, which shows how we learn about the world.

	Listening	Speaking	Reading	Writing
Learned	1st	2nd	3rd	4th
Used	Most (45%)	Next most (30%)	Next least (16%)	Least (9%)
Taught	Least	Next least	Next most	Most

When we communicate with people in a face-to-face setting we use two principal ways to transmit our message: words (voice tone and content) and body language. Our 'word message' is made up from the words spoken and the way words are spoken. The 'body language message' is what we project through our gestures, actions and the way we dress.

You might have thought interviews are all about talking, and assessments of candidates will be based purely on the words they say. However, a number of studies have shown that the majority (about 70–80 per cent) of the messages we transmit to other people come through our body language. The interviewer will be looking for body language that is open and relaxed rather than closed and tense, and will respond better to someone who looks him or her straight in the eye rather than moving their gaze in other directions – which can look shifty. (To find out more about body language, see the publications recommended at the end of chapter 7.)

DURING THE INTERVIEW

In many interviews you have a maximum of 30 minutes in which to create an impression. Research by Robert Half International, a major international recruitment firm, sought to discover how quickly recruiters made their decision: results for the UK, shown below, might come as a shock.

Time reach a decision	UK respondents
Less than 1 minute	1%
1–10 minutes	32%
11–20 minutes	24%
21–30 minutes	16%
31–40 minutes	3%
41–50 minutes	5%
51–100 minutes	6%
More than 100 minutes	3%
Don't know/NA	10%
Average (in minutes)	22.8

As you can see, almost 90 per cent of decisions are made within 30 minutes. And according to other research, employers' impressions are made up in the following way:

- body language and image (70 per cent)
- tone of voice (20 per cent)
- what you say (10 per cent).

From the moment you enter the room you are being judged and measured. The impression you create in the first few seconds is crucial and can set the tone for the rest of the interview.

If the interviewer offers a hand, smile and shake hands firmly. Wait to be invited to sit down. If the wait seems too long, ask, 'Where would you like me to sit?' If you're offered a drink, accept it. Even if you take only one or two sips, it will be very useful if your throat starts to dry up.

Remember, you are well on the way to a job offer. The interviewer hopes you are the right person. Take a few deep breaths, relax and be natural. This is your opportunity to show the interviewer that you are the person for the job.

Sit well back in your chair, in an upright but comfortable position. If you use your hands when talking, be aware of it and do not overdo it. Make friendly eye contact with the person asking questions. Do not stare. If you feel uncomfortable holding eye contact with people, look at the point of their forehead just above the nose – it works. If there is more than one interviewer, make sure you also involve that person by addressing the next part of your answer to them.

Use the interviewer's first name only if invited to do so.

For panel interviews or interviews with more than one person, address the main body of an answer to the questioner, but then hold eye contact with other panel members in order to involve them. Panel interviews and other selection methods are discussed later in this chapter.

Brevity is the essence of good communication. Pause briefly to think before you speak. Do not ramble, wasting valuable time. The interviewer is more interested in the quality of your answer than the quantity. Avoid talking too much about your early career: it is your recent achievements that are likely to be most relevant. This is especially important for older candidates. The interviewer probably may not have been born when you started out in your career. As interesting as it may be, the interviewer does not need to hear your life history. Focus on the experiences and achievements of the past five to ten years at the most.

Listen actively to what is being asked or said. If you need to get a better understanding, repeat or rephrase the question. It is far better to do this than to spend time answering a question that has not actually been asked.

Be prepared for questions the interviewer knows you will find difficult to answer, such as ones about a controversial subject or difficult situation. These are asked to see how you respond under pressure. Do not blurt out your answer: a short pause shows thoughtfulness.

Throughout, stress what it is about your skills and achievements that make you the person for the job. Introduce five or six key 'you' points that focus on your skills and achievements. Use real examples from your past career. Help the interviewers to see how your skills and experience will benefit their organisation. It will be too late if you remember when you are halfway home. If one of the interviewers is your potential manager, ask yourself whether you will be able to work with him or her.

Have a notepad and pen handy in your bag, pocket or briefcase to take notes of the answers to your questions at the end. This shows you have thought about the job. Questions you might like to use are shown near the end of this section.

THE TOP TEN THINGS TO AVOID IN INTERVIEWS

1 Showing references, job descriptions or samples of your work unless asked.
2 Criticising previous employers and long stories about why you left jobs, particularly if you had a grievance with a previous employer.
3 Talking about personal or domestic matters, unless asked.
4 Getting on your soap box. What you do in your own time is of little concern to most employers, but few like activists or shop-floor politicians at work. Practise courteous answers to any likely questions.
5 Mentioning salary/remuneration package. Let the interviewers know what you can do: this may well influence their view of what you are worth. Usually employers have a salary range in mind. If you ask about money too early they will give the lower figure. Just as people might go shopping to buy, say, a hi-fi system with a price in mind of £500–£650 only to end up buying one for £750, the same happens in recruitment.
6 Name-dropping: it can backfire.
7 Interrupting the interviewer in your enthusiasm to make all your points.
8 Pretending that you have a better offer elsewhere to try to push them into a decision. But do let them know if you are being interviewed by other people – it can sometimes

focus the mind. The interviewer will not want to miss out. Take care not to give away too much information (for example, the names of the other potential employers).

9 If you are a smoker, make sure you have your last cigarette a while before the interview so that the smell does not hang on your breath or cling to your clothes. Or try using anti-smoking chewing gum for a day – remembering to remove it before the interview.

10 Last but no means least, do not mention your age unless you are asked, and never be apologetic about your years. Focus on your **experience**, your **maturity** and your **skills** and **achievements**.

'I have met candidates who have said things like "I've served my time in jobs where you have to make tea and do filing – I'm not prepared to do that any more", not understanding that in *most* roles people have to make tea and do filing. Even our MD takes his turn with the tea! Also, job roles have evolved to become much more multi-functional, and roles like typist or filing clerk are disappearing as everyone does their own typing in a "paperless office", so an open mind is very much a prerequisite to finding the best available suitable job in the market.

'Candidates of any age can have an inflated conception of what they would like to earn because their last job had pay increases with length of service. This means nothing to your next employer, who will pay according to the job you are doing. Be prepared to take a (sensible, not silly) drop in salary for the right opportunity as you can soon build it up again once you prove your ability in the new role.'
(professional recruiter)

PREPARING FOR QUESTIONS

You cannot know what is going to be asked at an interview, but you can improve your chances by practising some common questions – ideally with a friend.

The most common question you are likely to face is 'Tell me about yourself'. If you answer it well you will create a good first impression which should put you in a positive frame of mind for the rest of the interview.

Tell me about yourself

Prepare for this one well before the interview, by writing a short 'Me' statement. In one or two sentences *briefly* outline your personal circumstances: *'I'm married to Gill. We have two sons who are at university and we live in Warminster.'* The interviewer is not interested in your collection of Beatles memorabilia, your passion for steam trains or your love of needlepoint.

After the personal snapshot make your first mini sales pitch: make five or six positive statements about yourself which focus on your work skills and achievements. You might want to cover three major areas, with examples of your work ethic/approach to work, how you work with others, and finally your skills and achievements. Rehearse and commit the short statement to memory.

When you are asked, try to sound as if you are speaking spontaneously rather than repeating something you have learnt.

Initial nervousness in an interview may cause you to say too much. Try to avoid this. If you are asked to talk about your career history and you have had a variety of jobs, do not dwell on your early career. The interview will have been scheduled to take a set amount of time and it will probably be more important to talk about current/most recent responsibilities and achievements.

Below are listed some of the recruitment interviewer's favourite questions, with some guidelines on answering them. Your answers should be honest, but designed to put you in the best light by demonstrating your skills, knowledge, achievements and experience. Avoid giving answers which are self-effacing or which undersell you a candidate. Also avoid any questions which might lead you to say anything which is less than complimentary about your previous employer, boss or colleagues.

Why did you leave your last job? (or) Why do you want to leave your current employer?

No matter what the circumstances, never be derogatory about previous or current managers, colleagues or organisations. It is much better to say that you believe that you have realised your potential and are looking for a new opportunity or challenge.

Are you successful?

The answer has to be an unhesitant and unqualified 'yes'. Qualify the answer by giving a couple of examples from your personal life and three or four from your work life. Explain how you set goals for yourself and work towards achieving them. If you cannot answer this question positively you will do yourself no good at all. Employers want to recruit winners (not losers). The recruiter will be thinking: *'If you're 50+ and can't think of successes in your life, then when are you going to start being successful?'*

What do your colleagues say about you?

Be prepared with a quote or two from colleagues or your boss/ex-boss. Either a specific statement or a paraphrase will work well: *'My last boss used to say that I was one of the hardest workers she had ever known.'* The answer may make you blush, but interviews are no place for modesty.

What do you know about our organisation?

If you have done your research this should be easy. Focus on two or three positive things that you have learned about the organisation, which show why you are interested in working for them.

What have you done to develop your skills/improve your knowledge in the past year?

Focus mainly on activities that relate to the job. Organisations like to employ people who are flexible and keen to learn. If you cannot answer this question, or your answer is 'nothing', you may be shooting yourself in the foot. A learning log is a good way to remember what you have learned over the year: why not put one together for the past 12 months? See Appendix II for an example.

Are you a team player?

Yes. Have two or three examples ready which show how you have contributed to the success of effective teamworking in the past. Even lighthouse keepers have to work well with others, and teamworking is a key element of many workplaces.

Have you ever had to fire anyone? How did you feel about that?

If you have ever fired someone you will probably agree that terminating someone's employment is one of the toughest situations which any manager has to encounter. On the one hand you are taking away the employee's means of earning a living and depriving them of a good deal of dignity. On the other hand you are releasing your company from a contract with an employee who is failing to meet the required standards of working, or who is behaving in an unacceptable way. Be serious and factual in your answer and most of all keep the actual circumstances confidential. Talk about how you did what had to be done but took no pleasure in your responsibility.

What would you bring to our organisation?

You should be eager for this question. Summarise what you can bring to the organisation as well as what working for the organisation would do for your personal development. Do not be modest: this is your chance to 'sell' yourself.

What are your greatest strengths?

Do not be stuck for words. Be positive. If you have done the CSI–SADI questionnaire from the 'Personality and behavioural evaluations' section on pages 89–94 or the Keirsey Temperament Sorter (see page 105) the answer should come easily. Remember, you were asked for your greatest strengths so pick five or six, chosen to relate to the job and match what you think the employer is looking for.

The following list might help: a good listener, a natural leader, a natural planner, a perfectionist, a team player, an achiever, analytical, assertive, businesslike, cautious, challenging, competitive, confident, conscientious, controlled, co-operative, decisive, deliberate, determined, direct, disciplined, exact, focused, friendly, goal-centred, helpful, independent, logical, non-aggressive, non-confrontational, opportunistic, organised, patient, personable, positive attitude, practical, quality-focused, quick off the mark, sensitive, straightforward, structured, supportive, task-oriented, trusting, understanding, taking the initiative. Recruitment definitely is not an area where 'one size fits all'.

What would your previous boss say your greatest strength is?
This is a variation of the last question. How about adding in a sprinkling of these: creativity, drive, energy, enthusiasm, expertise, hard worker, initiative, leadership, loyalty, patience, positive attitude, problem-solver, team player, tenacity.

Remember, the interview is a selling situation – you need to sell yourself positively (nobody else will) without being pompous or arrogant. Older candidates often undersell themselves, so focus on your answers to these two questions and think about examples from your past that demonstrate your personal qualities and skills.

What is your greatest weakness?
Never say that you do not have any – we all have them and not being able to recognise that shows a degree of self-awareness. That said, you do not have to 'confess your sins'.

If you say something to the effect that you get frustrated when you have to work with people who are prepared to accept low standards, people who do only just enough to get by, or people who constantly criticise their employer, you will effectively turn the question on its head. (See also the next question.)

What kind of person would you refuse to work with?
This is loaded to see whether you are a team player and whether you get on with others. This time, instead of saying that you do not like shirkers or whingers, move to a higher ground, and say that you would have difficulty working with people who are disloyal to the organisation, violent people or people who discriminate against others.

What motivates you to do your best at work?
Your response will be entirely personal but might include: challenge,

achieving goals, being recognised, working for a fair boss, being stretched, and learning new skills.

Would you willing to work overtime? Nights? Weekends?

Be completely honest – there is no point saying you would just to get the job, then trying to re-negotiate when you start.

Would you be willing to relocate if necessary?

You should obviously discuss this with your family prior to the interview, if you think there is a chance it may be asked. Answer honestly.

Describe your leadership style

'I've never really thought about it' or *'I just let people get on with it, and tell them to come to me if there's a problem'* just is not good enough. If you are applying for a supervisory or managerial job that involves leading others you might need to learn a bit more about leadership styles. See end of chapter 7 for suggestions on further reading.

If you were recruiting a person for this job, what would you look for?

Make sure that you mention the skills and knowledge that are needed, and which you have.

Don't you think you are overqualified/too experienced for this position?

This is a common question for older candidates who have decided to apply for a job which is less senior or carries less responsibility than their previous job, and is potentially discriminatory (see page 144). Talk about the challenges and the job satisfaction that you anticipate from a change of direction. Be positive and enthusiastic. The interviewer is probably concerned about a number of things: will the job be too boring for you, or will you come in and start trying to change everything? If the interviewer is potentially your new boss he or she might feel daunted because you are more qualified and experienced than they are. Help them to feel comfortable with the situation.

What qualities do you look for in a boss?

You are on safe ground if you say something like: *someone who is skilled and knowledgeable, someone who has a good sense of humour, is fair and loyal to subordinates and someone who sets high standards.* Most bosses think they embody all of these traits.

What is your work ethic?

Stress how your work ethic will benefit the organisation; determination, high standards and loyalty are a good start. What else could you add?

These are just some of the questions you might be asked. There are many others.

Try answering some of the questions shown below. Paint the best image of yourself and show what you have to offer by talking about your skills and achievements.

Are you being interviewed for any other jobs?

Are you seeking employment in an organisation of a particular size? Why?

Are you willing to travel for the job?

Describe the best job you've ever had.

Describe the best boss you've ever had.

Describe the most rewarding experience of your career so far.

Have you ever been dismissed/disciplined? Tell me about it.

  [Tell them what you learned from the experience]

Have you ever been fired or forced to resign?

Why did you leave [name of organisation]?

Can you explain this gap in your employment history?

Have you ever had difficulty with a supervisor? How did you resolve the conflict?

How would you describe your career progress to date?

How are/were [name of organisation] as employers?

What did you enjoy doing at [name of organisation]?

What have you learned in your time with [name of organisation]?

How is your health?

How many days' sick leave have you taken in the last two years?

How do you determine or evaluate success?
How do you plan to achieve your career goals?
Do you have plans for continued study? What are they?
How do you take direction?
How do you work under pressure?
How well do you adapt to new situations?

What area of work do you feel least confident about?
What motivates you to go the extra mile on a project or job?
How would you evaluate your ability to deal with conflict?
Give an example of a major problem you encountered and how you
    dealt with it.
What have you learned from your mistakes?
What two or three things are most important to you in your job?
How would a good friend describe you?

In what kind of work environment are you most comfortable?
What are the qualities of a good leader?
How well do you work with people? Do you prefer working alone
    or in teams?
Are you good at delegating tasks?
What are the qualities needed in a good [job title]?

What are your expectations with regard to career development and
    salary increases?
What are your long-range and short-range goals and objectives?
What are your long-range career objectives?
What are the most important rewards you expect in your career?
What criteria are you using to evaluate the company for which you
    hope to work?
What do you expect to be earning in five years?
What do you see yourself doing five years from now? Ten years
    from now?
What have been your greatest achievements?

*What two or three accomplishments have given you the most
  satisfaction? Why?*

*What's more important to you – the work itself or how much you're
  paid for doing it?*

*What have you accomplished that shows your initiative and willingness
  to work?*

What do you really want to do in life?

What interests you about our products/services?

What do you think it takes to be successful in a company like ours?

What do you know about our competitors?

What makes a good employer?

What makes you qualified for this position?

What qualities do you look for when recruiting people into your team?

What's one of the hardest decisions you've ever had to make?

Which is more important: creativity or efficiency? Why?

Why did you become a [job title]?

Why did you choose this career?

What have you been doing since you left [name of organisation]?

Do you have any hobbies? What do you do in your spare time?

What's the most recent book you've read?

How do you relax?

How do you spend your holidays?

Why should we offer you this job?

COMPETENCY, CRITERIA-BASED OR BEHAVIOURAL INTERVIEW QUESTIONS

There is a method of recruitment interviewing called criteria-based, competency or behavioural interviewing (all different expressions for the same thing), which attempts to take an objective approach to recruitment.

Some interviewers ask hypothetical questions along the lines of

'Older workers are no different to workers of any age in terms of being selected for a job. Everyone is expected to prepare in advance, have undertaken the appropriate research and be able to give examples in a criteria-based interview. Being able to provide concise and relevant answers in a criteria-based interview is quite a challenge for anyone who is not accustomed to this style of interviewing, so many employers encourage prospective applicants to practise this.'
(Elaine Bromberg, Diversity Manager, HSBC Bank plc)

'How do you think you would react in [situation]?' This might be: 'What would you do if two of your sales representatives started a relationship?' or *'What would you do if you found that an employee had been fiddling their expense claims?'* Here you find yourself second-guessing the interviewer by saying how you would behave, in the way you think they want to hear.

Past performance is the best predictor of future behaviour. Competency or behavioural interviewing is based on this philosophy. Interviewers ask questions about what you have done in the past, since this is their best indicator of how you may perform in the future. They are trying to find out if you have handled situations in a positive way and whether you have learned from experience.

Help them by:

- describing the situation and what had to be done
- explaining what you did
- describing the outcome in positive terms.

Keep your answers brief and to the point.

Prior to the interview, the interviewer will have assembled a variety of questions from the following 'dimensions' to use in the interview to see if you match up to the requirements. Some candidates are completely lost for words when asked this kind of question. Avoid this situation by thinking in advance about the skills-set needed for the job in question. Practise answering some of the questions below. They seem simple but are really very searching.

Adaptability
Tell me about a time when you changed your priorities to meet others' expectations.

Describe a time when you altered your own behaviour to fit the situation.

Tell me about a time when you had to change your point of view or your plans to take into account new information or changing priorities.

Client focus
Give an example of how you provided service to a client/stakeholder beyond their expectations. How did you identify the need? How did you respond?

Tell me about a time when you had to deal with a client/stakeholder service issue.

Describe a situation in which you acted as an advocate within your organisation for your stakeholder's needs where there was some organisational resistance to be overcome.

Communication
Describe a situation you were involved in that required a multi-dimensional communication strategy.

Give an example of a difficult or sensitive situation that required extensive communication.

Tell me about a time when you really had to pay attention to what someone else was saying, actively seeking to understand their message.

Decision-making
What are the most important decisions you have made in the last year? How did you make them? What alternatives did you consider?

Describe an occasion when you involved others in your decision-making. To what extent did you take notice of their input?

Developing others
Tell me about a time when you coached someone to help them

improve their skills or job performance. What did you do?
Describe a time when you provided feedback to someone about their performance.
Give me an example of a time when you recognised that a member of your team had a performance difficulty/deficiency. What did you do?

Effort/initiative

Tell me about a project you initiated. What prompted you to begin it?
Give an example of when you did more than was required. Give an example of when you worked the hardest and felt the greatest sense of achievement.

Interpersonal skills

Describe a situation where you wished you had acted differently with someone at work. What did you do? What happened?
Can you describe a situation where you found yourself dealing with someone whom you felt was over-sensitive. How did you handle it?
What unpopular decisions have you recently made? How did people respond? How did that make you feel?
What are some of the most difficult one-to-one meetings you have had with colleagues? Why were they difficult?

Innovation

Describe something you have done that was new and different for your organisation that improved performance and/or productivity.
Tell me about a time when you identified a new, unusual or different approach for addressing a problem or task.
Tell me about a recent problem in which old solutions wouldn't work. How did you solve the problem?

Impact and influence

Describe a recent situation in which you convinced an individual or a group to do something.
Describe a time when you went through a series of steps to influence an individual or a group on an important issue.
Describe a situation in which you needed to influence different stakeholders with differing perspectives.

Leadership

Tell me about a time when you had to lead a group to achieve an objective.

Describe a situation where you had to ensure that your actions spoke louder than your words to a team.

Describe a situation where you inspired others to meet a common goal.

Have you been a member of a group where two of the members did not work well together? What did you do to get them to do so?

What do you do to set an example for others?

How do you work as a team member? Give examples.

How would you describe yourself?

Organisational awareness

Describe the culture of your organisation and give an example of how you work within this culture to achieve a goal.

Describe the things you consider and the steps you take in assessing the viability of a new idea or initiative.

Tell me about a time when you used your knowledge of the organisation to get what you needed.

Planning and organising skills

What did you do to prepare for this interview?

How do you decide priorities in planning your time? Give examples.

What are your objectives for this year? What are you doing to achieve them? How are you progressing?

Problem-solving and judgement

Tell me about a time when you had to identify the underlying causes to a problem.

Describe a time when you had to analyse a problem and generate a solution.

Tell me about a situation where you had to solve a problem or make a decision that required careful thought. What did you do?

Relationship-building

Describe a situation in which you developed an effective win/win relationship with a stakeholder or client. How did you go about building the relationship?

Tell me about a time when you relied on a contact in your network to help you with a work-related task or problem.

Give me an example of a time when you deliberately attempted to build rapport with a co-worker or customer.

Resource management

Describe a situation in which you took a creative approach to resourcing to achieve a goal.

Tell me about a time when you had to deal with a particular resource management issue regarding people, materials or assets.

Describe the options you would consider to resource a project or goal if you did not have the available resources within your own span of control.

Describe a situation in which you established a partnership with another organisation or stakeholder to achieve a mutual goal. What steps did you take to ensure the partnership was effective?

Results orientation

Tell me about a time when you set and achieved a goal.

Tell me about a time when you improved the way things were typically done on the job.

Describe something you have done to improve the performance of your work unit.

Describe something you have done to maximise or improve the use of resources beyond your own work unit to achieve improved results.

Sales ability/persuasiveness

What are some of the best ideas you ever sold a superior/subordinate? What was your approach? Why did it succeed/fail?

Describe your most satisfying (disappointing) experience in attempting to gain support for an idea or proposal

Self-management

Describe the level of stress in your job and what steps you take to manage it.

Describe a time when you were in a high-pressure situation.

Describe a time when things didn't turn out as you had planned and you had to analyse the situation to address the issue.

Strategic thinking

Describe a challenge or opportunity you identified based on your industry knowledge, and how you developed a strategy to respond to it.

Describe a time you created a strategy to achieve a longer-term business objective.

Describe a time when you used your business knowledge to understand a specific business situation.

Teamwork

Tell me about a time when you worked successfully as a member of a team.

Describe a situation where you were successful in getting people to work together effectively.

Describe a situation in which you were a member (not the leader) of a team, and a conflict arose within the team. What did you do?

CREATE YOUR OWN LUCK

Practise your answers to these questions in front of a mirror or with a friend/partner who is prepared to give you some feedback. It will feel a little uncomfortable but it is worth it, because it does work. Role-play may not be real life but it is as near as we can get, and just as professional singers rehearse and footballers train before matches, practising interview technique will help job candidates to deliver a good performance.

Use a tape recorder or, better still, a video camera to hear/see yourself as others do. You may not like what you have recorded, but you can use it to improve.

Practice pays dividends. When the American golfer Arnold Palmer was close to winning the American Open and needed a final putt to win, he sank the putt and a spectator remarked on how lucky he had been.

Palmer replied that every day he spent two hours practising his putting and then said: 'It's a funny thing, the more I practise the luckier I get.' Practise your interview skills and you too can 'sink that putt' and get the job you want.

YOUR TURN FOR QUESTIONS

You sense that the interview is coming to a close. The interviewers have bombarded you with lots of questions and you feel that you have answered them pretty well. You are exhausted and looking forward to walking out of the building and relaxing. Then one of the interviewers says, 'Do you have any questions?'

In your eagerness to leave, your instinctive reply might be 'No, I don't think so'.

But interviews are a two-way street, and not having anything to ask the interviewer is a great mistake. It sends out a message that you are uninterested in the job or the organisation, or you are lazy and cannot be bothered to think about the position on offer, or that you are desperate and will take anything. Asking trivial questions is just as bad ('Does the coffee machine make cappuccinos?' or 'Will I get a desk with an outside view?' will do you no favours).

One thing worth knowing about a job vacancy is how it came about. Has a new job been created as a result of a re-organisation, or is the organisation expanding hence creating a new job? Or was the previous incumbent fired? Or did he or she leave because they could not stand the pressure of the job? Or because they hated working for the manager – like the other four people who left the same department last year? Clearly this is an area for diplomacy and tact, but knowing why people have left in the past can provide an insight into what it might be like to work for the organisation.

Questions such as 'How long does the induction process take? I'm really keen to start making contribution as soon as I can?' and 'What type of projects will I be able to help with?' show that you are thinking positively about a future with the organisation and are keen to make a start.

Open questions will help you to find out about the organisation: for example, '*I have seen the organisation's mission statement on your website. How does the mission statement get translated into day-to-day working practice?*' or '*How would you describe the culture of the organisation?* '.

135

You can ask questions which put you on the same level as the interviewer, as a prospective colleague, by questioning the interviewer in their capacity as an employee. For example: *'What attracted you to join the organisation?'* or *'How long have you been here?'* If it is a relatively short time, you can ask them about their first impressions. If it is a long time, ask what it is about the organisation that has kept them there.

Any questions about the organisation's finances, budgets or overall performance will give the impression that you have keen business sense (even if you do not). Also, it shows that you are talking to the interviews as equals.

Over the past years many organisations have flattened their management structures, losing levels of managers or supervisors, so be careful about asking about promotion prospects. It is much better to focus on how the job will develop and what opportunities you will get for skills development.

Make a note of questions you want to ask beforehand. When the interviewer asks if you have any questions, produce your notebook or notepad and take brief notes of the answers. Do not be concerned that the interviewer will think you are 'showing off'. On the contrary, they will be impressed that you have thought about the job and done some preparation.

Further examples of the kinds of information you might like to gather (but not all at once) are provided below, but you should spend some time brainstorming your own questions. Have a really good think about what it might be like to work in the organisation. What concerns do you have? What information have not you been able to learn from the organisation's literature or website? Sift out the questions that are important to you and do not be afraid to ask them.

QUESTIONS ABOUT THE JOB

What will be my daily responsibilities/duties?

What is the level of the job within the company's grading structure?

To whom does the post-holder report?

What are the main priorities?

What are the reporting lines, up/down/sideways? Are there any dotted-line responsibilities?

What will be my budget availability?

What will be my goals/targets/priorities?

What are the key relationships with other departments?

What are the people like in the team that I will be leading?

Are there any 'management' issues?

What is the team working on at the moment?

When can I meet the other team members?

Could I look around the office/store/factory?

What will be my first major priority?

What was the greatest achievement of the last person in this job?

What changes would you like to see in the way the job is performed?

How will the organisation commit to my training and development?

What are the opportunities for progress/career advancement?

What resources would I have available to help me achieve my goals?

What can you tell me about my boss?

QUESTIONS ABOUT THE ORGANISATION

What is the UK/total turnover (financial)?

Is there a mission statement? What is the organisational vision?

What is the company's profitability compared with competitors/budget?

How big is the workforce? What is the annual percentage of staff turnover?

What does the range of UK services/products comprise?

What is the company's e-commerce strategy?

How will this affect the future shape of the organisation?

What new products/services are under development?

What innovative ways are used to market your products/services?
What are your strategies for growth?
Where will the organisation be in five or ten years?

PRACTICALITIES (QUESTIONS FOR WHEN YOU ARE ON THE HOME STRAIGHT)

Is a medical required?
How soon do you want someone to start?
How is the pension scheme structured? Can you transfer in?
Where does the salary figure offered fit in on the salary scale?
(If they want to start you at the bottom of the scale, ask why.
Can you use your years of experience/skills to justify being started higher on the scale?)
What are the salary reviews based on and how often do they take
   place? When will the first one be?
Is there a bonus scheme, and, if so, how is it structured?
Are share options available?
Is there a car allowance?
What has been the average salary increase over the few years?
How are salaries reviewed?
What is the annual holiday allowance?
Is private healthcare available? How much does it cost? Are
   partners/family covered?
What sort of insurance scheme does the company have?
I'd like to be as effective as possible, as quickly as possible: is there
   any literature or other information that I can read in preparation
   for my first day?

Remember, the recruitment interview is a two-way process. You may be making a choice about where you will spend a significant part of your working life. Make the most of your opportunity to find out what you need to know and also to create a business-like impression.

Start with questions which show an interest in the job, not what the company can do for you. Above all, do not make your questions sound like an interrogation. Ask questions in a way that show your enthusiasm for the job.

Make the conversation flow. For example: '*I have read the job description. Can you tell me more about the job in terms of my major priorities and responsibilities?*' (Many job descriptions are a catch-all and the reality is that 80 per cent of your work will be covered by two or three of the responsibilities.) '*What type of training will I get? How do you see me fitting in to the role? How will I know how I am performing?*' Listen to the answers and try to make the discussion as natural as possible.

Note the use in these questions of 'will' rather than 'would': 'What *will* I be doing?' etc. rather than the hypothetical approach of 'What *would* I be doing?' It might seem like a minor difference, but is significant: 'will' is positive and suggests that you are already thinking about yourself working in the role, whereas 'would' is much more cautious.

ENDING THE INTERVIEW

Before the interview ends, find out how well you have performed, by asking for some feedback. If you are sensing that things have gone really well and you believe you have established the right level of rapport, you may feel confident enough to ask whether the interviewers will be inviting you back for the next stage or offering you a job.

On most occasions, simply saying 'What is the next step?' sends out a positive signal that you are interested in the job and you want to be considered as a serious candidate. It also helps you to clarify exactly where you are in the recruitment process.

Some recruitment processes can be long-drawn-out, comprising lengthy interviews with, perhaps, a recruitment consultant, then the person within the organisation to whom the job-holder will report, then presentations by shortlisted candidates to a panel, followed by a couple more interviews with senior personnel. This process can take some weeks, which is why it always worth checking the timetable.

Be sensitive about the interviewer's time. Ask pertinent and sensible questions and ask the questions in an enthusiastic way that says to the interviewer: 'I like the look and sound of your organisation. I want to know more, because I believe that I'd like to work for you'. Do they see you making a contribution to the team? Have they any reservations at this stage as to your ability to do the job? If they have reservations, this is your opportunity to prove that you are the person for the job. Is there anything else about you that they would like to know?

At the end, thank the interviewers for their time and say that you look forward to hearing from them. This confirms your interest in the job. As obvious as this sounds, candidates do sometimes forget.

And afterwards, relax and congratulate yourself on having been as well-prepared as you could be. Reflect on how the interview went and jot down key points which could be important if you are invited back for a next interview. You will probably have to wait to hear the decision, but you can learn from the experience.

Were you happy with the way you handled yourself? Did you say what you wanted to say? Did you find out what you needed to know? How many of your 'you' points did you get across? Was your behaviour positive, assertive, humble, tense, laid-back, talkative, controlled, etc.?

If you have been put forward by a recruitment agency, call as soon as you can to let them know how you got on and to confirm your interest in the job. The agency will almost certainly feed this straight back to the interviewer and it will be received positively. Otherwise, leave the ball in the court of the interviewer. Do not become too despondent if you do not hear for a while – recruitment can sometimes take several weeks. If, however, the recruiter promised to let you know, one way or the other, by a certain date and that day comes and goes, there is no harm in telephoning to see how soon it will be before you hear the decision.

Try to stay positive. You have years of experience. You have skills and maturity. The interviewer would not have wasted their time inviting you to the interview if they did not see you as a real potential candidate. They want to fill the job vacancy and they are hoping that you are the right person for the job, just as you are hoping to get the job. Never let yourself think that you have no chance because you are an older candidate.

If, ultimately, you are rejected, remember that the likelihood is that this will happen quite a few times before you get the job offer you crave. Try to put it down to experience, analyse what you could have done better, and look forward to the next opportunity in a positive frame of mind. Maintain your self-belief, never undersell yourself, continue to prepare thoroughly and practise before interviews, and you will eventually win through.

INTERVIEW CHECKLIST

Do

✔ believe in yourself, your abilities and what you can offer
✔ practise common interview questions in advance
✔ dress to impress
✔ switch off your mobile phone
✔ organise important papers, work samples etc. beforehand
✔ make a positive impression quickly
✔ listen actively and concentrate
✔ maintain eye contact
✔ smile when appropriate
✔ speak confidently and clearly
✔ take time to think about your answers
✔ avoid 'yes' and 'no' answers
✔ ask if anything is not clear

Don't

✘ go to the interview smelling of garlic, alcohol, cigarette smoke or overpowering perfume or aftershave
✘ dress too casually, or wear too much/inappropriate jewellery
✘ take a friend, relative or pet with you
✘ enter the interview room laden with bags
✘ sit down until you are offered a seat
✘ slouch or sit defensively with arms and legs crossed
✘ greet the interviewer as casually as you would your friends
✘ waffle or avoid questions
✘ ask about bonuses, holidays, coffee breaks

✔ be enthusiastic

✔ give honest answers

✔ give positive answers

✔ keep salary expectations within the advertised range

✔ keep to the point – do not ramble

✔ have your own questions ready, and make sure that the questions you ask are relevant

✔ send a thank-you letter or an email

✔ keep in contact with the recruitment agency, if appropriate

Above all, **do** have faith in yourself and your ability to do the job.

✘ ask negative questions (such as 'What happens if I can't increase sales?')

✘ brag about how many interviews you have lined up

✘ criticise your present or past employer

✘ fidget or play with your hair, clothing, mobile phone, items in your pockets, etc.

✘ get into discussions about your personal life

✘ give negative answers such as 'I don't know' or 'I'm not sure'

✘ interrupt the interview to take a phone call

✘ play it cool by showing little enthusiasm

✘ show that you are desperate for a job

✘ stop the interview early to go to another one

Don't undersell yourself or believe that you haven't got a chance.

TELEPHONE INTERVIEWS

Employers sometimes use this method for screening candidates prior to inviting them to a one-to-one interview.

If a recruiter calls you, make sure that you take the call in a room where there are no distractions. Have your CV, the job description, company information, and pen and paper ready. Treat the interview in exactly the same way that you would treat a face-to-face one. Stand up – it will give you more confidence and that will come across in the tone of your voice. Relax and speak clearly and concisely. If there is a silence, do not be tempted to fill in. Telephone interviews can be daunting, especially if this is your first experience of one.

Make sure your voice is pleasant and personable. The recruiter cannot see you and is trying to build a mental picture of you. Sell yourself just as you would in a face-to-face interview. Whatever you do, never give a telephone interview on the hoof, while you are in the pub or travelling, or indeed or anywhere where you cannot give the interview your undivided attention.

PANEL INTERVIEWS

Panel interviews are designed to improve decision-making and minimise the risk in recruitment. Part of the objective for some of them is to see how you can cope with pressure.

Panels normally consist of three to six people but can comprise as many as a dozen for some types of position. Each of the interviewers will bring something different to the panel, and each will have an agenda to satisfy with their questions. Panels often sit in a horseshoe formation, with the interviewee's seat in the middle at the front. The prospect of being 'interrogated' by a number of people in such circumstances can be extremely daunting, but there are techniques for getting through them.

Try to identify the key figures on the panel. The chairperson is easy to identify as he or she will normally make the introductions; listen very carefully to who's who. Identify the person for whom you will be working – this person will be the one you most need to impress. If there is a panel member with whom everyone else seems to agree, try to impress that person.

Maintain eye contact with the individual who asks you a question, but also include others in your answer; end your answer with the person who originally asked the question. This method ensures that each member of the panel is encouraged to listen to your answer and provides an opportunity for you to establish rapport. Remember to smile and convey enthusiasm at all times – even though you may feel scared to death. If you feel completely intimidated and wish that the ground would swallow you up, try imagining that every one of the panel members sitting in front of you is naked and sitting on a lavatory. The mental picture this conjures up may not be attractive, but it is a technique that works because it helps you to feel in control.

INFORMAL INTERVIEWS

There is no such thing as an informal interview. If you are asked along for an informal 'chat' then by all means be pleasant, friendly and sociable; but remember the stakes are still the same as if it were a more formal interview. Prepare for the interview in exactly the same way as any other interview and expect to be asked the same sort of questions.

DISCRIMINATION IN INTERVIEWS

Employment decisions should of course be made on grounds of competence to do the job. Discrimination is unlawful. The employer should not be selecting on the basis of age, and your aim should be to emphasise the advantage of your experience.

However, if you are 64+ and the organisation has a mandatory retirement age of 65, you will be at a disadvantage.

If you do not get the job and genuinely believe that you have been discriminated against on grounds of age, there are number of things you can do. Make a note of any ageist remarks that have been made, including references to your being 'over-qualified' or 'not fitting in' – perhaps with a younger workforce, or a line manager who is younger and less experienced than you.

Ask for feedback on the interview, with reasons on why you have not been appointed, and look for evidence of stereotyping or discrimination. (Again, the publication *How to Recognise Cases of Age Discrimination*, available at www.taen.org.uk/publications/ad_guide_for_workers.pdf, could be useful: see especially page 44.)

If you feel you have evidence of discrimination, you could write to the managing director or chief executive of the organisation, as the person who discriminated against you may have acted totally against policy. You could go to Citizens Advice or an employment lawyer and look at the pros and cons of lodging a formal case.

Or you could simply put it behind you and move on to the next opportunity. Only you will be able to decide which is the most appropriate course of action.

HSBC no longer asks candidates their age on their application forms, dates for qualifications, schooling and work experience. HSBC has also gone through a screening process with the recruitment agencies that it uses. It examined the agencies' standards on diversity and reduced the number from 228 to 50 so that they are easier to monitor.

CIPD report: Age and Recruitment. www.cipd.co.uk

PERSUASIVE PRESENTATIONS

Many organisations ask candidates to give a presentation as an additional 'interview' method. This is also the most common assessment centre exercise (see next section). The recruiters/assessors will be looking for you to communicate your message effectively, for you to project yourself confidently, and for you to know what you are talking about. They will also be trying to gauge how much work you have put into the exercise and how seriously you took it. Sometimes you will present to a panel of recruiters alone, but some companies include other candidates in the audience. If you are asked to sit in on other people's presentations, try to think of a couple of searching (but not intimidating) questions. Also, take some notes on how you objectively rate the performance of the other candidates.

Most people find knowing where to begin is the most difficult step. For the moment, resist any temptation to switch on your PC. Instead, follow the following structured method for designing a successful presentation.

1 Ask yourself, 'What do I want the audience to learn or do as a result of my presentation?'
2 Write this objective in the middle of a blank page
3 Now let your mind 'freewheel' to produce a mind-map or spider diagram of ideas (see below)
4 You will find that you have far too many things to say, so next you need to edit and give the presentation some structure

(The mind-map below was drawn by the author before the first draft of this section was written.)

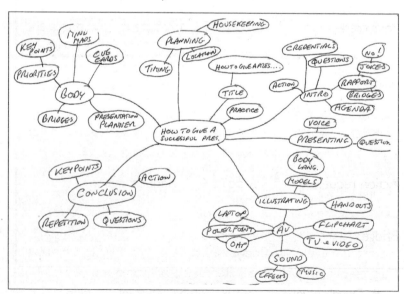

5 Use the headings in the presentation planner below to help you to structure your talk
6 Look at your mind-map and choose the most important point which you want to communicate

7 Write this on the presentation planner as **key point 1**

8 Add the other key points in descending order of priority:
key points 2–5. Resist any natural tendency to save the best
until last, given that people are most attentive at the start

PRESENTATION PLANNER

Introduction (develop this section second)	Main body (develop this section first)	Conclusion (develop this section last)
Rapport statement	Key point 1	Remind audience of the problem/opportunity
Presentation subject	Bridge	
Your credentials	Key point 2	Restate the key points and crystallise the message
Agenda	Bridge	
Question request	Key point 3 Bridge	
Action request	Key point 4 Bridge	Request action
Bridge	Key point 5 Bridge	

9 Develop your content by putting other information
from your mind map into your key points, using only
information that is relevant to achieving your objectives

10 Limit your key points to a maximum of five (three is
even better).

You have now developed the main body of your presentation. But before moving on, decide how you will link or create a **bridge** from one point to the next. A phrase such as 'Now let us look at the introduction' lets the listeners know you have finished one topic and acts as a signpost to what comes next. Other useful bridges are: enumerating ('First . . .', 'Second . . .' etc.) when you have stated that you have a specific number of points to cover; 'On the contrary . . .' or 'On the other hand . . .' when you are weighing up pros and cons; or simply 'Next . . .'. To avoid sounding hackneyed, use a different bridge to move from each of your key points.

11 Write the bridges on your presentation planner.
12 Write the introduction

Use the headings from the presentation planner to help you to develop a short **introduction**. You have only one opportunity to make a first impression. So how do you create that positive impression from the start? The first step is to establish empathy by building a bridge to as many audience members as you can. If you can do so, speak informally to each person before you begin. When you stand to address the group, reinforce the bridge by saying how much you have been looking forward to meeting them ... and pay some compliment to their office, factory, etc. (**rapport statement**). Do not start with a joke: you never know whom you may offend and alienate.

Now say what you are going to talk about, seen from their viewpoint (**presentation subject**). But why should they listen to you? You should say a few words here about why you are qualified to speak on this topic, what you have done to research the subject, what your background is in this field, etc. Two or three sentences establish your credibility (your **credentials**).

Now give the audience a 'map' or **agenda** of what you will be talking about. The agenda is simply a list of the key points which make up the body of the presentation. Signal that questions are permitted ('*As we go through the presentation please feel free to ask questions if I* *have not explained anything clearly – although we do have a few moments at the end for questions.'*). Telling people to save their questions until the end rarely works, so why not prepare for it? Doing it this way (**question request**) also signals to the audience that you are confident of what you are talking about. Next, state quite clearly what you want them to do as a result of listening to you (**action request**):*'When I've finished speaking I hope you will see that the strategy I am advocating will help to re-position [product] in the marketplace.'* Finally, your bridge: you need to link to the first key point in the presentation.

Your **conclusion** should be short and to the point, but not rushed. You want to encapsulate your presentation into a package that they can take away with them. **Remind** the audience of the **problem** or **opportunity**. Restate your **key points** and crystallise the message: this is really a reiteration of the agenda. **Request action** – what do you want them to do? *'I hope you now agree that the strategy I am advocating will help to successfully reposition [product] in the marketplace.'*

This structure for your presentation ensures that your key points are stated at least three times – and repetition is a very powerful persuader.

Now you have developed the content and structure of your talk you can decide to reinforce your message with visual aids.

MAKING YOUR POINT WITH POWERPOINT

PowerPoint is a tremendous tool for creating persuasive presentations. With a few clicks of a mouse you can bring a car, a crocodile or even Concorde into the room. However, you may be familiar with the expression 'death by PowerPoint': too many people confuse the medium with the message, and use all the bells and whistles of PowerPoint to create boring screen shows or confusing circus acts, with fade-ins and outs and all the other trickery. None of this will disguise low-quality content.

Here are some top ten tips for getting the best out of PowerPoint.

1 Use a consistent slide design with an uncluttered background for all your pages. (Menu Bar/View/Master/Slide

Master).The layout will then be consistent for all the new pages you create.

2 Use a consistent colour palette: do not start to fiddle around with the colours that are recommended in the font or text palette – they are there because they complement each other and do not clash.

3 Avoid page after page of bullet points and subheadings – words on a screen are not visual aids. Use short stab points. *Do not put your script on the screen.*

4 Use visual images every time you can. But avoid using the Microsoft clipart or sound files that came with your PC – your audience will have seen/heard it all before. If you 'search for images' using a search engine such as Google you can get images of almost anything. By clicking on your mouse you can save the image to your PC and then paste it into your presentation.

5 Include diagrams, graphs and flow charts – a picture is worth a thousand words. Better still, include a 10- or 15-second video clip (if you are using someone else's PC remember you will also need to copy the video file on to their hard drive and re-establish the link into your presentation).

6 When you have created the presentation ask, 'What can I edit out without losing the meaning?' Be ruthless: cut out everything that is not absolutely necessary.

7 Use only one font (sans-serif) throughout, such as Arial or Helvetica. If you want to emphasise a word, use font size, bold, italic or colour, but do not underline. And do not change the font to something obscure: you could find that when you load your presentation on to a different computer the slides will contain nothing but gobbledygook, because the font is not on the other computer.

8 When people look at a new slide, their eyes will move from the top left to the bottom right of the screen. Artists will tell you of the two-thirds/one-third rule for creating

balance in a picture. In a nutshell, put your visual 'bottom right' two-thirds down and one-third from the right.

9 If you use transitions, use the same simple one throughout until you want to highlight a change of subject or really emphasise a point.

10 Remember that each slide is part of a process. So when you have finished, run the slideshow to make sure that the sequence flows comfortably, and fits in with the 'story' which you developed using the presentation planner.

KEY POINTS FOR POWERPOINT PRESENTATIONS

- If you emphasise everything, you emphasise nothing.
- KISS – keep it short and simple.
- Whichever visual aids you use, follow the basic principles of keeping them as uncomplicated as possible.
- Use large letters and uncomplicated words as stab points so that they can be read easily.
- Do not write complete sentences on the slide.
- A picture is worth a thousand words.
- As a general rule allow 45 seconds to 1 minute per slide.

Rehearse your presentation once or twice so that you know what you are going to say and how you are going to say it – say the words out loud. Use a friend as a timekeeper and to give you constructive feedback.

Be prepared. When you go to your interview take a copy on a CD or a DVD and another copy on a memory stick.

ASSESSMENT CENTRES

Assessment centres or selection centres are used by a number of organisations to select people for jobs. They are very often called 'development centres' when used internally, to identify people with potential for development or promotion. Depending on the job, an assessment centre session can last from half a day to three days or more.

The event will usually be run by a chairperson who will facilitate a series of group exercises and tests and will manage the timetable. He or she will be observing the way everyone works together, forming an overview of the 'group dynamics'. Then there are the observers. They will have been trained and briefed before the meeting and will have studied your CV. Each observer will be allocated a person or people to observe, and will take copious notes and 'mark' the performance of these candidates. Part-way through the assessment observers may switch candidates in order that a better-balanced view is obtained.

After the assessment centre event finishes for you, the real work of the chairperson and observers begins. The chairperson facilitates a process by which each candidate is individually evaluated against the pre-set performance standards, to make the selection process as objective as possible. These meetings can last for many hours. The panel's decision will be based on what they have learned about you during the assessment centre. So how can you outshine the other candidates and demonstrate that you are the best person for the job?

Get lots of sleep beforehand and try to arrive refreshed. Assessment centres will burn up your adrenaline reserves – and more. It is highly likely that, just as you are starting to relax, you will be handed a mammoth task with a tight deadline to see how you respond under pressure: for example, candidates might be given a task at 10pm (straight after dinner) with the requirement for a report to be delivered at 8.30am the next day.

Observe the performance of the other candidates. You may be asked to rate their performance. Be prepared to give a factual and analytical summary of their contribution. Do not be afraid of criticising other candidates, or praising them, but make sure that what you say is based on fact. You may be asked to rank the performance of all of the candidates (including yourself).

If you have been invited to join everyone the night before the assessment event, do not assume that the assessors are off-duty. They will probably be assessing your social competence over dinner, in the bar, or over breakfast.

Think through the qualities the assessors will be looking for and how you can demonstrate them: for example, leadership, interpersonal skills, ability to handle stress, verbal and written communication, flexibility, negotiation skills, problem-solving, commercial acumen, decision-taking, initiative and creativity.

Do not try to suppress other candidates in an attempt to make the assessors notice only you. You will come across as overbearing and insensitive.

EXERCISES

Assessment centre exercises measure you against aspects of the job. For each exercise, make sure you understand the chairperson's instructions or the written brief. If you do not understand, ask. Not listening and not reading instructions thoroughly are the two biggest mistakes made by candidates. The following are common exercises.

Presentations

See the previous section for tips on how to prepare your presentation. This is the most common exercise. The assessors will be looking for you to communicate your message effectively, project yourself confidently and know what you are talking about. They will also be trying to gauge how much work you have put into the exercise and how seriously you took it.

Sometimes you will present just to a panel of recruiters, but some organisations include other candidates in the audience. If you are asked to sit in on other people's presentations, try to think of a couple of searching (but not intimidating) questions. Also, take some notes on how you rate the performance of the other candidates.

Sales or negotiation role-play

You are asked to sell a product or negotiate a deal.

Ask probing questions: how? why? when? where? what? and which?

are best for gathering information. Listen to the answers and try to match the needs of the customer with what the product does. As an example, one of the all-time favourites when recruiting new salespeople is for the interviewer to say, 'Sell this fountain pen to me'. Unenlightened candidates immediately start prattling on about style, design, gold nibs and good ink flow. The smart ones ask questions such as 'Do you use a fountain pen?', 'What qualities are important to you when you're choosing a new pen?', 'What would you expect to pay for a fountain pen?' And then they will go on to match the product's features and benefits to customer needs.

People who do badly in these exercises do so because they are too busy putting over their own viewpoint, based on assumptions, rather than asking questions to find out what the customer wants.

Business simulation

This may be paper-based or computer-based. You are split into small groups and over a series of rounds compete with other groups to develop, manufacture, market and distribute products.

Play to win. Think strategically. Aim to establish a long-term viable business with a robust product portfolio.

Invest in research for new products in the early rounds – products do not last forever.

As you get results back at the end of each round, analyse the performance of the competitors – you may be able to undercut them or market your product to a niche.

(See also the interpersonal skills aspects of the next section.)

Group discussions (interactive skills)

You are given a problem to solve as a group. Common problems are simulations where your group has been stranded at sea, in the desert or on the moon. Being detected is the first priority, followed by food. Also, work out which items you have that can be used as signalling devices.

Formulate your own ideas quickly and sell them convincingly to the group.

Suggest that the group needs a structure and timetable to work to, and propose one. Do not steamroller other people's ideas: listen attentively.

If someone is not contributing, draw them into the group by asking for their ideas.

Five minutes before the end, suggest that you need to summarise your decision and take control, or suggest that someone takes control, of whatever needs to be done.

RECRUITMENT TESTS AND EVALUATIONS

Some organisations use tests and evaluations in their selection process. Before inviting people to interview, the recruiter identifies the personality traits, skills and knowledge which the ideal candidate would possess. During the selection process candidates are asked to complete tests to evaluate whether they possess these qualities.

The extent of the testing can vary from a five-minute form-filling exercise through to a whole day involving a battery of tests and evaluations and an interview with a psychologist. Whatever the format, take the tests in your stride, do your best and be honest.

Personality questionnaires are another technique. As their name implies, these questionnaires aim to gain an insight into personality. Usually there is no time limit for a personality questionnaire, but you are advised not to over-analyse your reply and to move quickly from question to question. Do not answer questions as you think you should: be honest, otherwise you will be defeating the object. Also, some personality questionnaires have an in-built evaluation to check to see how consistent (honest) your answers have been.

The most commonly used personality questionnaires are the Myers-Briggs Type Inventory (MBTI), reputedly the most widely used one in the world; the SHL Occupational Personality Quotient (SHL OPQ); the Sixteen Personality Factors (16PF); and one by Thomas International. There are many others.

Skills and aptitude tests, unlike personality questionnaires, are designed to test you against standards. The most common ones are numerical, verbal and abstract reasoning tests.

Numerical tests identify the ability to pick out and manipulate key information from tables, graphs and semi-technical reports.

Verbal tests identify the ability to pick out information from reports and then make objective decisions based on the information in the text.

Abstract tests examine the ability to think flexibly. They measure the ability to recognise order in the midst of apparent chaos, to focus on certain aspects of a task and to ignore irrelevant detail.

Your score in the tests will be compared against 'norm' tables to see how you have performed in comparison with previous groups of people who have taken the test.

You will find examples of the kind of questions you will face at the websites of SHL and ASE: details in chapter 7.

Attending an assessment centre usually involves at least one interview, and sometimes candidates are interviewed by a number of different people.

If you are applying for a line management job you might be given an overview (hypothetical or real) of the team you will be taking over, and some of the management issues you will be faced with, and asked to give a short presentation on how you would handle them. Think and read in advance about strategies for handling poor performers, and read about leadership skills (see publications list at the end of chapter 7).

For a strategic marketing job you might be asked to carry out a market analysis and write a marketing plan showing how you would launch a new product, or re-launch a failing one. Brush up on some of analytical tools such as SWOT, PEST and force-field analysis.

An assessment centre event is a tremendous opportunity for you to show what you can do. Be positive, be prepared to play the game and use every opportunity to show that you have the qualities needed for the job. ■

5

EMPLOYMENT MATTERS

EMPLOYMENT MATTERS

This chapter offers tips on staying employed – fitting into your new organisation, knowing your rights, and knowing how to stake your claim if you believe you have been wrongly or unfairly treated.

MAKING A GOOD IMPRESSION – AND KEEPING YOUR EMPLOYER IMPRESSED

When you start your new job you will be on the same starting blocks as any new employee. Your new employer will be watching how you settle in, hoping that you will become a productive member of the workforce as quickly as possible. Try to make a positive first impression.

You have already impressed your new boss during the selection process. Now it is time to show that you can live up to expectations. Work on building a good relationship. Identify his or her working style and standards. Find out what is important to them.

As well as your punctuality and how you dress, your performance, behaviour and the quality of your work will be under scrutiny. Like all new employees, you are being watched closely – by colleagues as well as your boss. Labels are sometimes applied very quickly and last for a long time. Set the standards: if you are a supervisor and unhappy with the quality of someone's work, address the issue quickly and tactfully. If you are pleased with people's work, say so. Everyone likes praise.

Ask your boss for feedback. Ask 'How am I doing?' at the end of your first day and again at the end of your first week. If you ask too frequently it may look as if you are not confident, but if you strike the right note you will impress your boss with your enthusiasm for receiving feedback.

By all means bring in new ideas, but do not get stuck in replay mode.

If your new organisation does not have an induction programme, ask for one or at least ask if you can be introduced to the key people with whom you will be interacting in the course of your work.

WAYS TO ALIENATE COLLEAGUES
– AND YOUR NEW EMPLOYER

- Keep talking about what a good organisation your previous was
- Make excuses for your age: *'You can't teach an old dog new tricks'* or *'You'll have to forgive me – I'm not as young as you'*
- Treat colleagues/co-workers in a condescending way because they are younger than you
- Refer to yourself as the 'old fogey' (or similar), or refer to your colleagues as boys and girls
- Keep making suggestions, in a critical or abrasive way, on how things can be improved.

When you look at these statements in the cold light of day they look like such obvious mistakes that you would think nobody would make them. But they do.

Take Peter. He is a brilliant painter and decorator with superb technical skills. He has been a painter and decorator since he left school, is past retirement age and is still going strong. His colleagues on the building site cannot stand him. They call him 'Eno' (He Know) – because Peter criticises the work of everyone, from plumbers to bricklayers. Peter has worked on so many building sites throughout his life that he feels qualified to comment on everyone's work. He knows everything, or so he thinks, and does not hesitate to advise others.

When you start your new job, you will be a complete stranger to your colleagues and only slightly less so to your new boss. Be sure to get off on the right foot.

Never shirk. Accept new challenges with enthusiasm. Clockwatchers, '9-to-5ers', people who spend a lot of time attending to personal or social matters, and those who shy away from work are likely to have a short shelf-life.

LEGAL RIGHTS AT WORK

The laws that protect people in the workplace have never been stronger. They have given all of us the benefit of improved quality of life at work, particularly in terms of equality.

Employers have what is known as a 'duty of care' towards their employees. They are responsible for providing good, safe working conditions and treating their staff decently – fairly, and without discrimination or harassment.

An employer who fails in these responsibilities is likely to have broken the law. Employees may have a case against the organisation and could be eligible for compensation.

Many employment law issues can be nipped in the bud, simply by raising them and discussing them with your employer. It may be that the breach of employment law was committed unwittingly, because the employer was unaware of their responsibility. Sadly, the vast majority of managers pick up their understanding of employment law as they go along and receive no specific instruction on their responsibilities. Compare this with driving a car: receiving the keys, being shown how to start the vehicle, accelerate and change gear, but having to work out the rules of the road by trial and error and watching other drivers. Accidents – on the road or in the workplace – are the likely result.

Nowadays, the sheer volume of legislation that impacts on the workplace represents quite a challenge for employers. It includes: the Control of Substances Hazardous to Health Regulations, the Data Protection Act, the Disability Discrimination Act, the Disability Rights Commission Act, the Employment Relations Act, the Freedom of Information Act, the Health and Safety at Work Act, the National Minimum Wage Act, the Race Relations Act, the Protection from Harassment Act, the Sex Discrimination Act, the Welfare Reform and Pensions Act, the Maternity and Parental Leave Regulations, Minimum Wage Regulations, Working Time Regulations, the Work and Families Act, the Employment Equality (Age) Regulations and the Human Rights Act, together with special regulations covering different workplace environments. In addition, the employer may have to adhere to the procedures and codes of practice specific to the profession or industry.

While most employers who break the law may do so unwittingly, others are aware of what they do and hope that they will not be caught. Just as most car drivers at some time or other exceed the speed limit and get away with it, organisations may take calculated risks that they can infringe employment law without being challenged.

The existence of a law does not mean that employers will take notice of it, as a glance at the newspapers will often reveal. Organisations do get taken to court, or to tribunal, by employees, and are often found guilty.

DISCRIMINATION AT WORK

Many organisations now operate 'equal opportunities' policies to ensure the fair and equitable treatment of all job applicants and employees. These should ensure that the organisation selects its staff on an objective basis (especially skills and experience), promotes mutual respect and embraces diversity.

Whether or not your organisation has such policies, discriminatory practice in the workplace is unlawful and there are steps you can take to combat it.

AGE DISCRIMINATION

If you believe that because of your age you are being marginalised, are missing out on training or promotion opportunities, or that there is a campaign to 'ease you out', you can invoke the law to protect you.

Although some exemptions are allowed under the Age Regulations, it is now generally unlawful for companies and organisations to treat employees and job candidates differently because of their age. It is also unlawful to deny training and education to people on grounds of their age.

The Employment Equality (Age) Regulations Act 2006, which covers England, Scotland and Wales, and the Employment Equality

(Age) Regulations (Northern Ireland) Act 2006 ban decisions about employment based on age.

Workers are now protected from:

- harassment in the workplace
- being overlooked for promotion
- lower salaries
- poorer benefits
- being dismissed
- being refused a job
- being made redundant

on grounds of age. They are also protected from being victimised for supporting a person with an age discrimination claim.

Also, age cannot be used as a reason for preventing future opportunities, including:

- training opportunities, which often lead to promotion, and
- pay rises.

Whether you are a job applicant, a full- or part-time employee, former employee or even self-employed working on contract, you have a legal right not to be discriminated against.

The age legislation should ensure that employers take action to prohibit age discrimination, and have suitable policies and procedures. If, however, you feel you have been discriminated against, you have legal grounds to challenge the organisation through its own grievance procedure. If necessary, you can move on to mediation, arbitration (in cases of unfair dismissal) or an employment tribunal.

Retirement

It is now unlawful to have a Normal Retirement Age (NRA) below 65 for employees unless an employer can demonstrate exceptional circumstances. However the Government has decided that it is lawful to set an NRA of 65 (known as the National Default Retirement Age) or above or to have no NRA. This is currently subject to challenge and, if the courts were to find that the aims of the NRA were not legitimate or the impact disproportionate, this important part of the Age Regulations might have to be changed. In any event, the arrangements are being monitored and will be reviewed in 2011.

SEXUAL DISCRIMINATION

The Sex Discrimination Act 1975 made it illegal to treat people differently in the workplace because of their sex.

Sexual discrimination means treating someone unfairly or unequally because of their sex. For example, employers are not allowed to pay a woman doing the same job as a man at a lower rate. But fair treatment goes well beyond pay and bonuses: it applies to recruitment; the way employees are treated at work, their opportunities for promotion and training, dismissal criteria and selection for redundancy. For example, employers may not select people of a particular sex simply to ensure that all members of a team are of the same gender, or use the argument that a woman (or a man) would not fit in. If they select using these criteria they will be breaking the law.

RACIAL DISCRIMINATION

The Race Relations Act 1976 makes it unlawful for employers to discriminate against anyone on the grounds of race, colour, nationality or ethnic origin. This applies to all aspects of employment: recruitment, selection for promotion, development, training, termination of employment, redundancy and so on.

The Act protects people against racial abuse and/or harassment and from being treated less favourably on grounds of race and employers have a duty of care to ensure that these rights are fulfilled. There are a very few circumstances where exceptions can be made.

DISABILITY DISCRIMINATION

The Disability Discrimination Act of 1995 applies to all organisations, no matter how small. It gives disabled people the same employment rights as everybody else. It covers selection and recruitment, day-to-day work, promotion, career development, redundancy and dismissal.

Approximately 8.5 million people in the United Kingdom (or 1 in 7 people) are disabled. The Act is designed to enable these people with disabilities to make a full contribution to the workforce.

GRIEVANCE PROCEDURE

By law your employer must inform you of its procedure for dealing with grievances. Normally your immediate manager is the person responsible initially for handling grievances. There must, however, be a formal procedure for taking grievances further.

There are two types of grievance: one where you may feel aggrieved about a situation, but there is nothing that can be done to change things. An example of this might be where you believe that you have been unfairly passed over for promotion, but in fact you did not meet the selection criteria. The best your manager can do is to help you to come to terms with the situation and then help you to look at career development and other opportunities.

In addition to discrimination, grievances could be about:

- terms of employment
- bullying
- pay and working conditions
- disagreements with co-workers
- sexual harassment
- physical violence
- being denied statutory employment rights.

Grievance procedures are designed to resolve problems at work. Depending on the nature of the grievance, you could try talking with your manager informally before using the formal grievance procedure, which is likely to follow the pattern described below.

Step 1: establishing your claim

Seek legal advice, from a trade union or legal advice charity, for example, as early as possible to ensure your claim remains in time.

If you are an employee, as opposed to a job applicant, write a grievance letter. A 'grievance meeting' will then be held, which could result in your being able to agree a solution with your employer without going to tribunal.

If the result of this meeting is unsatisfactory, you can appeal against the employer's decision, and ask them to reconsider. If the result is still not acceptable, the next stage is taking the issue to an employment tribunal, for which you may have to submit an application. It is important to act quickly and seek legal advice early on.

If you are not an employee (i.e. you were refused a job at recruitment stage) you should write to the employer, as outlined above, to try to resolve the issue and/or seek legal advice to file for an employment tribunal.

If you are a member of a trade union, it should be able to help. Otherwise, seek legal advice and support from one of the organisations listed in chapter 7.

Step 2: preparing a case

If you have exhausted the above and remain unsatisfied with the outcome, you can file the forms you need to launch an employment tribunal. An advice agency may help you with this process by issuing a questionnaire to the employer to which it must respond (failure to respond could be interpreted by an employment tribunal as unlawful age discrimination). Further information on how to take a case to an employment tribunal can be found at www.helptheaged.org.uk.

Step 3: alternative dispute resolution

All forms for an employment tribunal are forwarded to ACAS, an organisation that exists to champion better employment relations. ACAS will contact you to try to resolve the issue through mediation, or, for unfair dismissal cases, through mediation and arbitration. If mediation or arbitration is not suitable or appropriate, the case can progress to an employment tribunal.

Step 4: employment tribunal

The employment tribunal is the last resort for cases of discrimination. It is a public hearing at which you present your case and your employer responds to a panel of three people, including a legally qualified chair. You will have to submit evidence such as witness statements and supporting documents. You and your witnesses may be cross-examined by your employer (or their legal representative), and you may cross-examine your employer or their representative.

If the result at employment tribunal is unsatisfactory, you can appeal to an employment appeal tribunal.

Individuals may not have the support of a representative at an employment tribunal and community legal aid will not fund representation. However, some household insurance policies could cover legal fees and representation; alternatively, a trade union or other advice agency might provide representation at its discretion.

Representation may be provided at an employment appeal tribunal through legal aid if you meet the eligibility criteria.

If the employment appeal tribunal result is unsatisfactory, you may be able to take your case to the Court of Appeal.

In cases of unfair dismissal ACAS may offer arbitration, a hearing which takes place in private with yourself, your employer and a legally qualified arbitrator. Arbitration is entered into voluntarily, the decision is legally binding and there is no right of appeal.

You can find further guides for taking an employment issue through a grievance procedure on the government's website, www.direct.gov.uk. Further sources of help are listed in chapter 7.

DISCIPLINE AT WORK

Discipline at work is management-speak for the formal process of correcting an employee's unacceptable performance or conduct.

If you are being formally disciplined and have not read your organisation's disciplinary policy, now would be a good time. If your organisation has no disciplinary policy it cannot make up the rules as it goes along.

Contrary to what many employees and managers think, the objective of the disciplinary process is to improve the performance or the conduct of the individual, to the required standard. It is not meant to be a prelude to dismissal, but is about getting people back on track. The reasons for having a formal disciplinary procedure are for the protection and benefit of the employee, the manager and the organisation.

The disciplinary procedure is formal: it is not about the 'quiet word' a manager may have with an employee, nor is it a short, sharp reprimand.

There are many reasons why people might be disciplined at work. One is **poor performance**, which could mean:

- **failing to meet targets** Under-achievement against targets, such as not processing enough invoices in an accounts department, or not meeting production standards, having scrap rates of too high a level, etc.
- **failing to meet objectives** For example, under-performing in terms of budgetary restraints (overspending) or, for a sales person, under-performing by seeing too few customers over a given period
- **poor administration** Failing to submit weekly reports on time or incorrectly filing documents, for example
- **poor working relationships** Offensive behaviour towards colleagues, or apathy — such as non-participation in teamworking
- **poor productivity** Falling below the industry standard, perhaps in terms of the number of operations performed, articles produced, documents processed, service calls made etc.

Another disciplinary matter is **misconduct**. This could be in connection with one of the following:

- **absence** A series of short absences from work, or a long-term absence.
- **lateness** Persistently arriving late for work or arriving extremely late on one occasion
- **insubordination** Disrespectful behaviour or language to a manager (not necessarily your own manager) or a colleague
- **breach of confidentiality (non-deliberate)** Accidentally including confidential information in a letter to another customer or allowing a computer screen containing confidential information to be viewed by an unauthorised person
- **negligence (non-deliberate)** For example, failing to lock up on leaving the employer's premises when last to leave the building; allowing contamination of a batch of products, etc.
- **failure to observe procedures** For example, not completing timesheets, if required to do so, or inviting an unauthorised person into the employer's premises.

OPERATING STANDARDS IN THE WORKPLACE

Every organisation must have a set of operating standards. The operating standards should be written down and should have been communicated to you.

You will find the operating standards in a number of places, such as job descriptions, staff handbooks, contracts of employment and organisational policy documents.

The standards are normally communicated to employees through a variety of methods, including team briefings, organisational intranet, one-to-one discussion (including appraisals), formal documents, such as policy and procedures manuals, and less formal documents such as emails and memos.

Before you can be justifiably disciplined, the organisation must have set the standards, and these standards must have been communicated to you.

CORRECTIVE ACTION

If your manager has decided that your conduct or performance has started to fall below the required standard it is their responsibility as a manager to point this out to you and to agree with you how and when this will be corrected.

Whatever happens must be substantiated by factual evidence based on dates, times and actual behaviour.

The disciplinary process is formal and should be 'fair and reasonable' in the context of your organisation's culture and current working practices, and any agreed working practices with trade unions. Your employer has to follow a process that meets statutory requirements.

The following guidelines for employers, adapted from ACAS's *Code of Practice: disciplinary and grievance procedures*, will give you an indication of what the employer has to do before beginning a formal disciplinary process. If your employer acts inappropriately throughout the disciplinary process, fails to act in a fair and reasonable way, or dismisses you unfairly, you may have a case which you can take to a tribunal.

If your employer decides to institute disciplinary proceedings you are advised to read the full document (which is on the ACAS website) and if necessary take advice from your trade union, a Citizens Advice Bureau or similar.

INFORMAL ACTION

Cases of minor misconduct or unsatisfactory performance are usually best dealt with informally. A quiet word is often all that is required to improve an employee's conduct or performance. The informal approach may be particularly helpful in small firms, where problems can be dealt with quickly and confidentially. There will, however, be more serious situations, including ones where an informal approach has been tried but is not working.

If informal action does not bring about an improvement, or the misconduct or unsatisfactory performance is considered to be too serious to be classed as minor, employers should provide employees with a clear signal of their dissatisfaction by taking formal action.

FORMAL ACTION

Inform the employee of the problem
The first step in any formal process is to let the employee know in writing what it is they are alleged to have done wrong. The letter or note should contain enough information for the individual to be able to understand both what it is they are alleged to have done wrong and the reasons why this is not acceptable.

If the employee has difficulty reading, or if English is not their first language, the employer should explain the content of the letter or note to them orally.

The letter or note should also invite the individual to a meeting at which the problem can be discussed, and should inform the individual of their right to be accompanied at the meeting. The employee should be given copies of any documents that will be produced at the meeting.

(continued)

Hold a meeting to discuss the problem
Where possible, the timing and location of the meeting
should be agreed with the employee. At the meeting, the
employer should explain the complaint against the employee
and go through the evidence that has been gathered. The
employee should be allowed to set out their case and
answer any allegations that have been made. The employee
should also be allowed to ask questions, present evidence,
call witnesses and be given an opportunity to raise points
about any information provided by witnesses.

Decide on outcome and action

*(adapted from ACAS's Code of Practice: disciplinary and
grievance procedures)*

Q *How long do warnings last?*
A Just as when a criminal has served their sentence and a period of
time has elapsed, the crime is said to be 'spent', in a similar way disciplinary warnings do not stay on a person's personnel record forever.
  The following periods are considered to be good practice:

- verbal warning – disregarded after six months, unless the
  same offence is repeated
- first written warning – disregarded after 12 months unless
  the offence is deemed to be of a more serious nature
- final written warning – disregarded after 12 months unless
  the offence is deemed to be of a more serious nature.

Q *Can I be disciplined for two or more things at the same time?*
A Yes. Warnings in the disciplinary process are not like points on a
driving licence. You cannot automatically be given a first written warning because you started to produce substandard work when you have

been given a verbal warning for, say, persistent lateness. Each offence is regarded as a separate issue.

Q *Does my employer have to go through every stage of this process?*
A The short answer is no: in extreme circumstances where a serious offence has been committed an employer can go straight to a final written warning.

For example, when two engineers started to fight at work the ensuing investigation revealed that it was 'six of one and half a dozen of the other'. In some organisations they might have been dismissed for gross misconduct, but the employer took a more lenient view and issued each of them with a final written warning. However, the fight re-started less than a week later and they were both fired.

Q *What if I believe that I have been disciplined unfairly? Can I appeal?*
A If you believe that you have been victimised, treated harshly or disagree that there are grounds for being disciplined, you have a right to appeal to the next managerial level. Your organisation's disciplinary policy should explain how to lodge an appeal.

DISMISSAL OR DEMOTION
Dismissal should be within the terms and conditions of your employment contract (notice period etc.).

An alternative to dismissal is demotion to a position of less responsibility. Sometimes when an employee has been demoted and a period of time has passed during which wounds have healed, they have become motivated and effective employees. If you are going through a disciplinary process, feel that you are sinking rather than swimming and can see that there is a strong possibility of your being fired, it might be a good idea to see if you can negotiate a transfer to a job at a lower level.

GROSS MISCONDUCT
Gross misconduct at work almost inevitably leads to termination of

employment. Examples of gross misconduct are theft, gross insubordination (such as striking another employee), falsifying qualifications or references, fraud (including falsifying timesheets), malicious damage to equipment, arson and industrial espionage. People have also been fired for downloading pornography from the internet, and for a host of other reasons.

Summary dismissal

The consequence of gross misconduct is instant dismissal without notice or payment in lieu of notice.

(If an employer makes any payments in lieu of notice in the case of a summary dismissal they may have compromised their case at any subsequent employee tribunal.)

Q *Can I have a companion present at a disciplinary interview?*
A Since 4 September 2000 workers (contractors as well as employees) have had a statutory right to be accompanied at a disciplinary or grievance hearing.

This person can be:

- a fellow worker or
- a trade union official: even if your organisation does not recognise unions you have a statutory right to be accompanied by a trade union official if you wish.

Your employer should inform you of your right to be accompanied and you should inform your employer who your companion will be prior to the interview.

Fellow workers or indeed trade union officials do not have to accept your request to accompany you. A worker who agrees to act as a companion has the right to a reasonable amount of paid time to attend the interview, familiarise themselves with the case and to confer with you before and after the interview.

The companion's role is to support the worker. Prior to September 2000 the companion was allowed only to observe. Their role has now changed significantly. The companion:

- has a statutory right to address the panel/interviewer
- may not answer questions for the worker being disciplined, but may ask questions
- must be allowed to confer privately with the worker.

YOUR EMPLOYER'S RESPONSIBILITY

If your employer has decided to discipline you, they have a responsibility to do everything that they can to help you to get back on track, by offering training and support.

'Don't lose your job in the first place! Staying in is much easier than getting back in.

'Once out, look hard at the full range of your skills and knowledge. Don't assume that you can only go back into the same sort of job. Is this the chance to escape from a tired career track into something different? Can you offer an employer more than he is expecting?'

(Professor Stephen McNair, Director, Centre for Research into the Older Workforce, NIACE)

TERMINATION OF EMPLOYMENT

Most managers will not end someone's employment unless they have given the matter serious consideration and made rigorous use of the disciplinary process.

On the other hand, some managers are chancers and fire people without just cause in the hope that they will get away with it. This section will look at the grounds on which you can have your employment terminated and offer some advice on what you can do if you think you have been dismissed unfairly.

FAIR DISMISSAL

If you are the person being dismissed, it may seem to you that there is very little that is fair about the situation. But what the law means by 'fair' dismissal is dismissal with just cause.

There are five possible reasons whereby a dismissal may be fair:

1 capability or qualifications of the employee for performing the work of the kind he/she was employed to do.

Capability can include any assessment that refers to skill, aptitude, health or other physical or mental quality. Examples of this might be: a bookkeeper who in spite of adequate training constantly makes errors in calculations; a car sprayer who repeatedly produces poor work; someone who has been off work on long-term sickness; someone who has frequent short-term absence through sickness.

Qualifications could mean any degree, diploma or other academic, technical or professional qualifications relevant to the position held by the employee.

An employee's background could also act as a disqualification: for example, if a manager appointed by a brewery to run a public house by a brewery was subsequently found to have a criminal record, the magistrates would not be allowed to grant a licence to the manager. This would leave the manager unqualified to carry out their duties.

2 conduct of the employee: for example, a shop assistant who is aggressive, or abusive or indifferent towards customers; an employee who lied – perhaps about qualifications or previous experience – in their initial application to the company (the latter may be considered to be gross misconduct and the employee may be summarily dismissed).

3 redundancy of the employee's position (remember, it is the position and not the person that becomes redundant). For example, where a change in working practices means that the person's skills have become obsolete, such as a company who decides to switch its marketing methods from employing a direct sales force to using a website and direct mail. Another common cause of redundancies is the merging of two companies, whereby departments and functions would otherwise be duplicated. A third common cause of redundancy is the underperformance of the organisation, where reduced demand causes a reduction in production requirements and in turn the people needed to produce/deliver the goods or service.

(See also the section on redundancy rights on pages 182–4.)

4 inability of the employee to continue to work in the position held without contravention of a legal restriction or duty (in other words, because it would be unlawful for the employee to continue to carry out their duties). For example, being banned from driving would make it impossible for someone who drives for a living to continue in that role; a sales representative in a similar position might also find their job is at risk (the employer needs to take into consideration the length of the ban and whether the employee can make alternative arrangements, such as having their partner drive or hiring a driver at their own expense).

5 other substantial reasons such as a spouse being employed by a direct competitor or starting up a directly competing business, both of which could trigger a conflict of interests. (Although these situations could constitute a reason for termination of employment, they do not indicate automatic dismissal.)

EMPLOYMENT TRIBUNALS

If you believe that you have been unfairly dismissed or discriminated against you may take up your case with a solicitor, your union or through ACAS (Advisory Conciliation and Arbitration Service). This may lead to both parties attending an employment tribunal, although the case may well be settled before coming to tribunal (many are).

Tribunals were established by Parliament in 1965. They are less formal than courts of law. The process is designed to be user-friendly and you can make an application and represent yourself if you wish. Only the chairman is legally qualified, and he or she is assisted by two lay people, one chosen in consultation with employers' associations and the other with trade unions. Three-quarters of hearings at employment tribunals are for unfair dismissal.

Employment law expects organisations to act in a 'fair and reasonable' way. Fairness is the strongest test used at a tribunal. It attempts to assess fairness against the standards of another reasonable employer if faced with similar circumstances.

Complaints are made using form ET1, which is obtainable from employment offices, job centres or unemployment benefit offices, or online through the Tribunals Service, a government agency that can provide all the information you need for the process.

The tribunal will check that the claim has been made within the appropriate time period (normally months from the incident), and that it relates to a matter which can be handled by the tribunal. A local ACAS official will then normally become involved in an attempt to promote a settlement without having a hearing. Two-thirds of all cases do not go to a hearing, more than half being settled by means of conciliation – thus avoiding the expense in time and money of appearing at a tribunal. Other cases may be withdrawn after a pre-hearing assessment at which the tribunal receives written or oral representations by the parties, but does not take evidence. Otherwise, the case goes through to a full hearing, which is normally held in public.

The vast majority of decisions reached at tribunal hearings have been in favour of the employer, but that should not stop you if you believe you have a case.

The tribunal has powers to:

- award compensation
- order the reinstatement or re-engagement of former employees
- make recommendations about a range of employment practices
- make orders requesting compliance with various employment statutes
- make orders resulting from appeals against improvement and prohibition notices.

Employers like to avoid tribunals, not least because attendance at an employment tribunal is costly. A tribunal will involve attendance of your previous manager, the HR or personnel director or manager, the company solicitor/company secretary, and maybe others. It will obviously also have associated with it all of the preparation time for these people. Finally, if the employer loses it may be required to make a financial award to you.

In addition, the public relations dimension will weigh heavy with the employer. The press thrives on the 'David and Goliath' aspect of individuals who win against employers. The damage that can be done to an organisation's reputation or its standing in the local community is unquantifiable.

At one company, which had 'empowered' its managers to hire people without reference to higher authority, a manager interpreted this empowerment as meaning that he could fire someone. The employee won his unfair dismissal claim at an employment tribunal, and the case filled the front page of the local newspaper the following week.

If a company operates in an area of low unemployment and high skill shortage and is keen to recruit from the local community, it is obviously undesirable to have a high profile in the local press for unfairly dismissing someone.

If you decide to take your case to an employment tribunal your employer will have to satisfy the tribunal that the dismissal was fair.

In order to satisfy a tribunal that a dismissal was fair **the employer must:**

- demonstrate that the dismissal is for one of the reasons described above
- show that it acted reasonably in treating that reason as sufficient grounds for dismissal.

REASONABLE BELIEF

The tribunal is not expected to act as a court of law, establishing the guilt or innocence of an employer. The employer must show that it **acted reasonably** on the basis of information which it had at the time of making the decision to dismiss.

It must do this by demonstrating that it has followed the correct procedures to the letter and documented every aspect that it was possible to document. It must be able to demonstrate hard facts rather than just opinions.

EMPLOYMENT TRIBUNALS

The tribunal will want to know:

- whether there was a thorough investigation
- whether the employee was given a fair chance to discuss the matter
- whether there were any mitigating circumstances
- whether any previous warnings had been given, and if so how recently
- whether the dismissal was fair.

Q *My employer has said that they want me to sign a COT3. What is it?*
A Signing a COT3, a conciliated agreement, means that you will accept compensation instead of making a claim at an employment tribunal. Remember, the ACAS representative's role is as a conciliator – ACAS is neutral and sees the situation from both sides. If you have not already done so, you may wish to seek legal advice before signing the COT3, or at least talk to someone at a Citizens Advice Bureau.

Q *Is unfair dismissal the same as wrongful dismissal?*
A No, they are not the same and are based on two different sets of laws. You can claim for wrongful dismissal if there has been a breach of your employment contract (either oral or written) by your employer which led to your dismissal.

The most common example of a wrongful dismissal is failure to give an employee the correct length of contractual or statutory notice, or dismissing someone without adequate payment in lieu of notice.

Some dismissals are unfair, some are wrongful, and some can be both. For example, imagine that you have for been working as supervisor in a food factory for the past three years. You have a one-month notice period in your contract. You get on OK with your manager, but not much better than that: you tolerate each other, and recognise that you each become thin-skinned in the other's presence. You have never been disciplined for poor performance or misconduct. At last week's supervisor's briefing you disagreed strongly and openly with your boss about a new process she is introducing. Following the meeting, you were called to your boss's office, where she dismissed you, telling you that she had had enough, and you were to 'pack your bags and go'. She said that you would be paid up to the end of the week, but no more than that.

In such a situation, you would have the following claims: wrongful dismissal claim (relating to the salary and benefits for your one-month notice period), and unfair dismissal (because there appears to be no fair reason to dismiss, and because the manager has not followed the correct statutory procedure).

If you had been allowed to work your month's notice or paid in lieu of notice you would not have a claim for wrongful dismissal, but you could still claim for unfair dismissal as your boss did not follow the correct procedure.

REDUNDANCY

If you are going to be made redundant, you should be treated fairly by your employer, which would be expected to follow certain procedures.

You might also be entitled to a redundancy payment.

Redundancy is a form of dismissal from a job. Reasons for redundancy include: situations where: new technology or a new system has made a job unnecessary; the job you were hired to do no longer exists and there is no alternative available; your organisation needs to cut costs, meaning staff numbers must be reduced; or the organisation is closing down or moving to a location where it would be impractical for you to continue working for it..

Making people redundant is among the most difficult situations for any manager to have to handle, simply because external or organisational reasons are responsible for the job loss – not anything to do with the employee. As a worker, you could be the best PA, security guard, manager, assembly worker or whatever in the organisation, but once you have received that redundancy notice you will be as unemployed as anyone else – with all of the pressures that brings.

REDUNDANCY PAYMENT AND OTHER RIGHTS

Under the Employment Rights Act 1996 an employee has a right to receive a redundancy payment, subject to a qualifying period of two years' continuous service if they are dismissed because of redundancy. This normally also includes employees who are made redundant who have been continuously employed on a series of continuous temporary contracts for two years or more. Remember, this is the *minimum* statutory requirement. Many employers make payments in excess of the minimum requirement and others reduce the qualification time.

If you have two or more years' service you are also entitled receive the appropriate notice, time off to look for alternative work and in addition a trial period of up to four weeks working in any alternative job available within the organisation (without jeopardising your redundancy rights).

Redundancy must be 'fair' in the legal sense of the word: it must be genuine – employers may not use redundancy as a 'soft option' for an early retirement or for getting rid of you if you are underperforming. There must be no alternative work available to offer you, and your employer must follow the organisation's written redundancy policy.

Your organisation's redundancy policy should contain:

- a statement of their intention to provide job security as far as is possible
- details of the consultation process for involving employee and trade union representatives
- a statement of the measures which the organisation will take to avoid or minimise redundancies
- the selection criteria do not have to be based on length of service, or operate on a 'last in, first out' ('LIFO') basis. They may be subject to the retention of key skills, experience and knowledge. There may also be provision for an offer of voluntary redundancy or early retirement options to be made to employees before selection for compulsory redundancy begins
- details of severance terms including statutory payments and ex-gratia payments
- a description of the appeal procedure for anyone who believes they have been selected or treated inappropriately
- details of any help available to assist the redundant employee to find alternative work: time off to attend interview, training workshops, outplacement programmes, and so on.

For further information and advice, visit the government's website www.direct.gov.uk and search on 'redundancy'. The ACAS website also has useful tips (see chapter 7 for contact details).

REVENGE: A DISH BEST SERVED COLD?

When a company fired one of its sales representatives, he felt he had been unfairly dismissed. He 'disappeared' and could not be contacted, but mailed the keys to his company car back to the office with a note saying 'Now find it' (the car). Five weeks later it was found in the short-term car park at Heathrow Airport, having run up a huge bill.

Satisfying though this may have been for the dismissed employee, there are drawbacks to this sort of tactic. Not least, any new employer would be highly likely to check back with the previous employer about the individual's conduct, which with electronic communication is very easy to do. Such behaviour could prove fatal to a new job offer.

BEFORE YOU MAKE A CLAIM

A note of caution: if you have you ever tried to put the cork back into a bottle of champagne, you will know that it is virtually impossible. In the same way, you might find that if you start legal proceedings against your ex-employer you may find yourself being sucked into something that you do not want to be part of, and that is likely to cause you a good deal of emotional trauma and stress. Sometimes, even if you are in the right, it can be preferable to draw a line under an experience and move on.

One employee who believed he had been wrongfully dismissed took advice from top employment lawyers and had backing from his trade union. They said that if need be they would take the case to the European Court of Human Rights. The employee was told that the case could take up to about four years. He had to weigh up the possibility of four years of legal wrangling, along with the stress it would cause to himself and his family and the prospect that he might not win, against the possibility that he might win and receive a substantial settlement.

He decided that even though he believed that he was in the right he wanted to get on with his life and draw a line under the episode, which must have been a bitter pill to swallow, though understandable.

If you believe you have a case and want to challenge an employer's decision, consider using the three-step process: thinking, maybe and probably.

Have a look at the ACAS and Tribunals Service websites, as well as other written sources of help. If you belong to a trade union, contact it for advice. Talk to someone at your local Citizens Advice Bureau. If, when you have done the research and talked to people, you think you have a case, you may wish to fight the case yourself. This is not a good idea. Instead, seek advice from a solicitor who specialises in employment law. Many solicitors offer a free first session so that you can explain your case and they can advise on whether it would be worth pursuing. There are numerous no-win/no-fee law firms as well, but do shop around and make sure you understand their working terms, remembering that if you lose you could still be liable for out-of-pocket expenses. ■

6

CREATING YOUR OWN JOB: SELF-EMPLOYMENT AND OTHER OPTIONS

CREATING YOUR OWN JOB: SELF-EMPLOYMENT AND OTHER OPTIONS

'If everyone who has talked about starting a business actually went out and did it, the whole world would be self-employed. But most people would rather fantasise about it than do it.' *(Mark McCormack, author of* What They Don't Teach You at Harvard Business School*)*

The world of work has changed enormously over the past decades. Today, very few people will work for the same organisation for the whole of their working lives. More and more people are moving into generating their own income. According to the Department for Work and Pensions 3 million of us in the UK are self-employed and the rate of new business start-ups is higher than ever – currently 400,000 a year.

This chapter looks at different ways of generating your own income and the pros and cons of 'going it alone'.

WHY WORK FOR YOURSELF?

There are lots of good reasons for wanting to work for yourself: maybe you have a great idea and can see an opportunity to earn money from it. Maybe you want to work from home, because of family commitments or to make better use of the time you have previously spent travelling to and from work. Maybe you have been unsuccessful in your job search and have come to the decision that if nobody else will employ you, you will have to employ yourself. Or maybe you simply want to be your own boss.

If you do decide to 'go it alone' you will soon realise that working for yourself is not just another job. It's a way of life.

If you like a 9-to-5 routine and a regular salary you will find that things are very, very different. You will probably have to make a

'One of my major motives in becoming self-employed was the thought that no one was ever going to tell me when to retire: that would be my decision. If you are doing something you enjoy and gain fulfilment from most of the time, it seems to me crazy to change it for a different way of life for no good reason. . .

'Our current way of life and the opportunities we have to stay fit and healthy are better than they have ever been. My father was, literally, an old man when he was the age I am now. My generation has no need to replicate this. If we take advantage of all the opportunities available to us there is no reason why the majority of us should not lead vigorous and highly contributive lives well into our 80s and beyond. . .

'One of the emotional challenges for many mature people is that becoming self-employed is a last resort following long periods of failure to obtain employment. Their attitude towards self-employment is therefore negative, and this in turn generates failure. If we can motivate people to view self-employment as an exciting and fulfilling challenge they will no longer see working for someone else as an option.'

(self-employed man, 73, who started his own business 10 years ago)

number of sacrifices for the sake of the job. Your earnings might be lower than you anticipate: if the cash flow becomes a trickle, or dries up altogether, you will be the last one to get paid, if at all. Your working hours may well be longer than you have ever worked before, which means that you will not have as much time as you used to for family or leisure activities, and you could stretch your personal relationships to their limits, or maybe even beyond.

Are you prepared to give your all to the new venture? Dylan Wilk committed a whole year in 1995 to set up www.gameplay.com. During that time he said that he was constantly working 24/7: 'I was working every single second of every single minute. Sure, I had to give up a few things, like sleeping and eating, but I was willing to do that.'

Would you be prepared to make the same level of commitment? Could you do it? Would you want to do it?

KNOWING YOURSELF

What are your interpersonal skills like? An important part of being self-employed is about managing relationships: with your clients or customers, suppliers, employees or sub-contractors, your family, and your professional advisers (your bank manager, solicitor and account-ant). If your preferred working style is to lock yourself in an office and get on with your job, you might experience difficulties.

Do you need a kick to get you out of bed in the morning or do you bounce out as soon as the alarm goes off? Being your own boss takes a lot of self-discipline. There are likely to be many days when you will have to sit at your desk instead of going for a long lunch – or any lunch at all – or making business calls instead of reading the newspaper. Finally, do you enjoy wearing lots of different hats? Depending on what you do, you may end up doing your own marketing and sales, financial planning, bookkeeping, administration, personnel management, office cleaning ….The list goes on. If you work for yourself, and by yourself, you may have to do everything.

Have you got the right personality to become self-employed? We are all different. Some of us love the idea of independence, are happy to work alone and love the opportunity to make decisions. Others, on the other hand, need to work with others and like to share their decision-making. Your personality might influence the kind of work you do: for example, the first individual might be happy working as a self-employed salesperson where they spend much of the day alone, whereas the second person might be more comfortable working in an environment where they have the company and support of others (one example might be a self-employed hairdresser who rents a chair in a salon and works alongside others doing a similar job).

SELF-EMPLOYMENT PROS AND CONS

You may have to take a substantial financial risk. If you need to raise money to get started, you may need to re-mortgage your home or take on a business loan. Depending on how much or little work you get, you may find that your cash flow varies from a flood to a trickle. You will need a cash back-up so you can pay your bills while you are waiting for business to come in or waiting to be paid for work that you have done. Since you will have to pay your suppliers first, this means that sometimes you may have to stint yourself to keep your business afloat.

If you are self-employed and not working you are not making any money. You do not have a company benefits package, which means that it might be hard for you to go on holiday. Every time you take a day off, and whether the reason is sickness, household or family commitments, or personal pleasure, you lose potential earnings. Working for yourself also means that you will have to manage your own pension plan.

You can choose your clients or customers, but you cannot control their expectations or actions. If you do not produce work that matches or exceeds their expectations, or if you do something that offends them, you might not get paid. Have you ever sent a meal back in a restaurant or refused to pay for something because of shoddy work? Even with the best intentions in the world you may find that your customer has different standards and expectations from yours. Even if your work is up to scratch, it is one thing to do the work and another to get paid for it.

You may need to learn some new skills, such as bookkeeping and submitting quarterly VAT returns. You can learn to do these things yourself – there are some excellent bookkeeping programs available for the SME (small to medium enterprise) market; alternatively, you can hire someone to do the work for you (for example, a bookkeeper to do your regular bookkeeping and an accountant to do your certified annual statement). Running a business can involve an awful lot of paperwork, and if you are not careful you can find yourself spending more time on the business of being in business than you are on the work that attracted you to self-employment in the first place.

Working for yourself, despite all this, might be your dream come true. There are, after all, a multitude of positives. If you are working for yourself, there is a good chance that you will have chosen to do something that you enjoy: just imagine how good it will feel to get paid for doing something that you love to do anyway.

Being your own boss means that you will be in control of all of the decisions affecting your working life. You will create your own business plan, your quality assurance procedures, your pricing and marketing strategies – everything. From one standpoint, you will have job security: you cannot be fired for doing things your way. As you do all the tasks related to your work, you will learn new skills and broaden your abilities.

The other side of the equation is that if you are self-employed there will be no cap on your potential earnings, and many people do earn considerably more than when they were employees. And to a large extent you can keep what you earn. The fruits of your efforts are all yours, because you own the tree. You will call the shots: if you want time off work for any reason, you will not have to fill in a holi-day request (though you may have to arrange for someone else to be available to respond to your clients). You may be able to work with your life partner, jointly sharing and participating in something that you own, and potentially strengthening that relationship. You should be able to decide your working hours, working conditions and busi-ness location.

If you work from your home, your start-up costs and operating costs can be kept to a minimum, and you will save time and money on daily commuting. If the location of your work is not important (say, if you are a freelance writer or a consultant), you may be able to live wherever you want.

The main driver for starting a business is often 'freedom'. When you create your own job, you have more control over your life. If you work well alone (but get on well with others), can work long and hard, tolerate or even enjoy risk and stress, and cope well with potential failure, self-employment could be right for you. Clearly it is not for everybody, nor is it a decision to be taken lightly, but for some people it is the best thing they ever did.

If it is for you, there are a number of ways you can move into self-employment. You could buy an existing business, such as a guest house, which will have an established trading record and could theoretically be running and generating an income from day 1, or you could start your own guest house and take steps to attract first-time visitors. Another possibility might be to buy a franchise, in which case you would pay a large sum of money up-front for anything from a fast-food restaurant to a print shop to a carpet-cleaning company.

Now for a reality check: most new business ventures fail (although the success rate of franchises is very high).

A BUSINESS OR AN OCCUPATION?

A key consideration when starting a business should be whether you want it only to provide you with a 'here and now' income, or whether you also want to build a business that you can sell when you retire – or whether you want to do both. Just as property increases in value over time, so can businesses. If you buy a house and make some improvements you should get a return on your investment when you come to sell. The same is true of businesses. If you want to get a flavour of the huge diversity of business options available for self-employment, buy a copy of *Daltons Weekly* from your newsagent or have a look at the website www.daltons.co.uk.

PREPARING FOR SELF-EMPLOYMENT

To maximise your chances of success, thoroughly research your business concept, define your product and service and your target market, and plan how you will develop the business. Make sure that you integrate your career and life goals into your business plan. Tell yourself that you can and will succeed (look back at chapter 1 to remind yourself of the importance of a positive mental attitude).

Gather as much information as you can. The Department for Work and Pensions, via the Jobcentre, has an induction scheme for business start-ups that would be worth signing up for (see pages 196–7). The high street banks produce free information packs, some of which even contain software packages to help you to produce a business plan. You could spend a few hours visiting all of the banks on your high street to see what is on offer and how they can help: remember, they all want your business, and as the majority of us tend to stick with a bank once we have our accounts set up, they will regard you as a desirable customer. Banks often offer incentives to start-ups, such as low-interest loans and free banking. Collect and read all of the relevant free information you can.

Contact your local Business Link for free courses and information packs (see chapter 7 for details, and remember that face-to-face contact is always best).

Read books on self-employment: some suggestions are *Lloyds TSB Small Business Guide* by Sara Williams; *The Complete Small Business Guide* by Colin Barrow; *From Acorns: how to build your brilliant business from scratch* by Caspian Woods; *Start Your Business: week by week* by Steve Parks; *White Ladder Diaries* by Ros Jay (a personal account of starting a small business); and, for a shot of inspiration, read *Anyone Can Do It*, Sahar and Bobby Hashemi's inspirational story about the building of Coffee Republic, from an idea at the kitchen table to a multi-million-pound organisation with over a hundred UK outlets employing thousands of people,.

Talk to as many people as you can who run their own businesses: local restaurant owners, landlords, newsagents, etc. No matter what the business, the potential problems are usually the same – cash flow, marketing, obtaining supplies. If you want to find out what running a business is really like, there is no substitute for talking to self-employed people. You will also hear, no doubt, of the enormous satisfaction that comes from being self-employed.

Research, research, research – and be wary of others. Partnerships, even among 'best friends', often collapse because of disagreements.

Most important of all, talk your idea through with your partner, if you have one. His or her support is essential.

See 'Keys to success', pages 198–9, to test your resolve and see whether you have what it takes.

> 'I had no desire to be anything other than an employee so it came as a horrid shock to be retired and self-employed at 65. I am fortunate in that my old company let me continue as a consultant, and also because a former colleague and friend wanted to set up a consultancy, so we are now up and running and making money.
>
> 'While you're employed, hang on to your clients by looking after them well. Then, if the crunch comes – redundancy or forcible retirement – they will in all probability continue to do business with you, no matter what.' *(print consultant, 66)*

If, when you have gathered all of the information and are totally committed to the idea of going it alone, abandon your job search. You cannot do either of them half-heartedly. Having made your decision, you need to go for it.

MOVING OFF BENEFITS INTO SELF-EMPLOYMENT

If you are on benefits, you can get extra support to help you become self-employed. The Jobcentre has a comprehensive support package available to help people to start their business; it can advise you whether your benefits will be affected if you start your own business and tell you about any other support available. Jobcentres often offer a three-stage training course, delivered by self-employment specialists:

Stage 1 Awareness and assessment. This is a one-day course

with a business consultant to explore whether you have a business idea which is likely to succeed. It will give you a good insight into what it is really like to be self-employed.
Stage 2 Planning your business. You will receive support for a period of up to eight weeks to develop your business idea. You will receive guidance and training for setting up and running a business. At the end of this stage, you will have produced a business plan.
Stage 3 Test trading. This stage allows you to test out your business with the support of a business expert. Test trading can last up to 26 weeks.

The support from a business expert continues for up to two years after you have finished the programme and are trading independently.

The Jobcentre has a good deal of information, advice and practical support available, most of which is free. It covers everything from planning a business and raising finance to making sure you have enough to live on while you get your business off the ground.

Ask Jobcentre Plus for details of programmes which offer this training, including eligibility conditions and the financial support you can receive.

BUYING A FRANCHISE

Compared with other new businesses, franchises have a good track record of success, but that success is not guaranteed. Even franchises fail, and when they do you can lose all the money you put up initially. Really thorough research can prevent this happening, though – talking to as many people as possible, asking to see audited accounts, speaking to suppliers and customers, and asking for factual evidence of previous successes. If what you see and hear does not present a convincing case, just walk away.

If you are considering buying a franchise, visit the British Franchise Association's website for tips and access to a number of books and

DVDs (see chapter 7). The information on the BFA website is designed to help you to make a more informed choice about franchising. All of BFA's members have chosen to be vetted against a strict code of business practice: they endeavour to be good franchisors that can deliver the success that you want.

FREELANCE, CONSULTING, INTERIM AND TEMPORARY WORK

Many professional people work as freelances, consultants or on an interim or temporary basis. Becoming part of the 'talent market' frees them from being committed to a regular job but provides an income without the risk of starting a business or setting off in a completely different direction. Could this be an option for you?

Years ago, 'consultant' was a word that many people put on their CV to cover a period of unemployment. The world is now very different. Many organisations have taken the decision to concentrate on their core business and to outsource projects or buy in expertise as needed on an *ad hoc* basis. Improvements in employee rights and the rising cost of making staff redundant also mean that organisations are very wary of increasing head count by taking on permanent staff if they can avoid it. This creates a phenomenal number of opportunities for people who can be contracted in for short periods. Some people, especially in skill-shortage areas, keep busy through temporary work and interim management assignments gained through employment agencies.

If this kind of lifestyle appeals to you, start contacting recruitment agencies that specialise in temporary and interim assignments and build a relationship with a small selection of them.

KEYS TO SUCCESS

If you want to succeed in selling your expertise to others, whether as a consultant, a freelance or an entrepreneur, you need to be able to answer the following questions positively.

- Have you defined your vision of what success means to you? What do you want out of your working life?
- Do you have complete insight into your skill and knowledge set? This is what you are selling, and to succeed as a consultant you need to be very, very good at what you do
- What have you got that people will want to buy in? How will you add value to your client's organisation? What difference will you make?

It is important to convince yourself that you have something to offer: if you cannot convince yourself, how will you convince a customer?

Clarify what you are offering. Do not offer too much, otherwise you could confuse your potential customers. You cannot be a specialist and a generalist – people want you for your expertise.

Establish that the market exists: do your market research.

Prepare a business plan and a marketing plan: they are different.

Prepare a budget and a cash flow forecast (guidelines and even free software are available from your bank).

Decide what you are going to charge, and which sector of the market you are targeting. Aldi, Lidl, Kwik-Save, Asda, Tesco, Marks & Spencer, Waitrose, Harrods and Fortnum & Mason all sell groceries, but their products and prices are targeted at different market sectors. It is easy to under-price yourself in a desperate move to get work, but once you have worked for someone at a set price it is difficult to increase it. You may also have different prices for different markets. For example, a business consultant might charge a public or voluntary sector client very much less than he or she would charge a commercial organisation.

Pick your professional advisers. You will need an accountant and maybe a bookkeeper – shop around, and ask for recommendations.

Choose a name for your business and get a website address. You may find it easier to check what website names are available, and then choose your trading name. Try www.easyspace.com in the first instance to find whether your website name is available or www.nominet.org.uk

if you want to learn more about registering a UK website.

Establish how you are going to finance the start-up. Even if you can do it on a shoestring and you can win some business in your first week, it may be weeks, or even months, before the payments start to roll in.

Set up your 'office' space, even if it is the space under the stairs: you will need an operations centre.

Talk to your tax office.

Talk to a financial planning adviser about insurance, such as office contents and business vehicles, pensions, professional indemnity and public liability. Some insurers offer cover specifically for small businesses operating from the owner's home.

Get free advice on start-ups from your local Business Link.

Set up customer records and systems, such as credit and invoicing procedures. Establish your trading terms and conditions and draw up model contracts. This can all sound quite tedious, but is essential if you are going to be taken seriously.

The keys to running a successful business are straightforward:

- maximise your income by generating revenue through effective marketing and selling
- minimise your outgoings by controlling costs through budgeting and cash flow control. If you can do this you will make a profit – which is what it's all about.

By all means produce an attractive logo and some product literature, but never under-estimate the importance of networking: personal contacts are by far the most effective way of finding new business, especially for freelances and consultants.

OPTIONS FOR TEMPORARY, INTERIM AND PART-TIME WORKING

Temporary, interim and part-time working all offer the opportunity for flexible working and can fit well into a portfolio career (see pages 202–4); alternatively, they could be your only source of income.

Temporary and interim workers are often 'fire-fighters', hired on a short-term basis to resolve an issue, or they can be employed to cover for someone who is absent from work for a period, or while a search for a permanent employee is carried out; or they may be brought into an organisation for their expertise in a particular area, such as acquiring another company.

There are some substantial advantages to working as a temporary or an interim worker; often, the needs are immediate and you could start the day after the offer is made; and earnings are often higher than the normal rate for the job. Also, if you are really looking for a permanent job, temporary or interim working is a great way of getting your foot in the door. If an employer likes the way you work you might be offered a permanent job. Working as a temp can be like an extended interview process.

Part-time work is a good way of having a steady income but with more flexibility than having a permanent job. With a couple of part-time jobs you may end up earning more than you could in a full-time job. Smaller organisations with a need for your expertise might not be able to afford to hire you on a permanent basis. A part-time job for a couple of days a week might be a great solution for both you and the employer.

As an older worker you may need to take a flexible approach to working: temporary, interim and part-time working can give you the opportunity to get back in to work and, if you want it, the work could turn into a full-time job.

Most of the websites listed in chapter 7 feature part-time and temporary jobs. If you are looking for full- or part-time work as an interim, try the website of the Interim Management Association www.interimmanagement.uk.com or use a search engine such as Google to find the websites of agencies that specialise in supplying interims (for example, Russam GMS www.russam-gms.co.uk). These websites have a wealth of useful tips on how to go about becoming an interim manager.

PORTFOLIO WORKING

The days of the gold watch presented for long service are gone forever. Most people will have half a dozen careers by the time they retire. Many people are 'breaking the mould' of a traditional 9–5 workday by replacing or supplementing their income with a portfolio of other jobs, some of which might be well out of the ordinary.

Portfolio working means having a number of different jobs or types of work. There is nothing new about the idea. Before the Industrial Revolution many people had 'portfolio' careers, earning their living in a variety of ways – maybe growing and selling food through the summer months and then, through the winter, working as an outworker for a manufacturer, or making and selling things themselves. The Industrial Revolution changed things, as many jobs relied on people using a narrow set of skills in repetitive tasks. To a large extent this is still true for many jobs. Portfolio working can give you the opportunity to use a much wider range of your skills. Some of the work might be done as an employee, some on a self-employment basis.

If you find it dull to do the same job every day, have found it impossible to get a 'real' job in spite of all your efforts, want to supplement the earnings from a regular job, need to supplement your pension, or just want to keep yourself from being bored in retirement, portfolio working might be for you.

Use this checklist to get yourself started.

- Assess your hobbies and interests. What do you really enjoy doing? Make a list to see whether any of them could be turned into revenue-generating work.
- Review your career. What jobs have given you the most pleasure or job satisfaction? How have you chosen these jobs?
- Evaluate your skills. Write a list of the skills you have *and* enjoy using. If you are good at bricklaying but hate doing it, leave bricklaying off your list. Do not focus only on technical skills – look at other accomplishments,

such as communications and leadership.

- Evaluate the pros and cons. Having a portfolio career carries risks. List all of the positives, such as a better work/life balance, freedom, doing what you enjoy; then list all the negatives, such as financial insecurity, lack of belonging, having an uncertain future. Then weigh them against each other and make a decision.
- Write a plan. Include a list of possible jobs, prospective employers/customers, a weekly or monthly schedule, include plans for a home working environment, whether an office or a workshop, and a budget. Where will the cash come from? What expenses will you have?

You can do an online evaluation to see whether you could become a portfolio worker, by visiting www.creativekeys.net/portfoliocareertest.htm

EXAMPLES OF PORTFOLIO WORKING

David retired in his early 50s after a career in the army and wanted to supplement his pension. He took a part-time job making deliveries for a local firm and also, as he is a keen gardener and good at DIY, placed a few cards in local newsagents offering his services for maintaining gardens and doing household repairs. In no time at all he had a client base of mainly retired people who needed a bit of extra help. He now has more work than he needs and a waiting list of clients, so he may be giving up the delivery job.

Susan divides her time between working as a freelance trainer, writing magazine articles and painting pictures, which she sells in a local gallery.

Brian is a safety manager on an oil rig and Christine has a small antiques shop. They used their savings to buy an investment property and have a regular income from renting it to students. They also buy properties at auction which they develop and decorate, using professional tradespeople, then selling on at a profit.

Bob, who is a retired accountant, does the books for a small local firm one day a week and also buys job lots of more or less anything at auctions, which he then sells at car boot sales.

Bill and Doreen are 'officially' retired, but are far too active to stop working. They run their home as a B&B, and Bill buys antique furniture at auctions which he restores and then re-sells at auctions at a profit.

Kathleen is a skilled secretary and seamstress. She works as a part-time secretary and earns a significant additional income by making curtains and other soft furnishings.

Jeannette is a lecturer at a college of education, but has reduced her hours to one day a week so that she can devote the rest of her time to selling optical aids online.

After retiring from the armed forces, where he worked in employment liaison, Tom began working in career transition for the over-40s, assessing skills. He also works for personal injury solicitors, assessing injuries and disabilities.

Phil left a senior position in a large organisation to move to the country, become a consultant and spend more time on outdoor pursuits. Combining his love of the great outdoors with the need to sustain an income he took a course in building dry stone walls and now offers his services to local residents.

These are just a few examples, but the number of possibilities worth exploring is of course enormous.

STARTING AFRESH

Here are some income-generating activities to think about.

Household skills Can you wallpaper a room? Paint window frames? Make curtains? Mow a lawn? Fit a new kitchen? Clean a house so that it shines like a new pin? Or do any of the multitude of practical things that are needed to keep a home in order? There is probably a market for your skills right on your doorstep.

This is because there is a huge deficit of professionally qualified people with practical skills – plumbers, joiners, painters and decorators etc. A couple of generations of people have been through school without learning the carpentry/metalworking/domestic science skills that were taught in schools two or three decades ago. Also, the population is ageing. As people get older, even with the best will in the world they become less able to do the household jobs that require stamina and fitness or manual dexterity. If you place a few cards in the local newsagents' windows and do a good job for people at a fair price, you will almost certainly have a trail of people beating a path to your door, and a steady income.

Free holidays Your age will work in your favour here. Are you sensible and honest? Do you like visiting different parts of the country? Do you like animals? Are you prepared to do a little housekeeping and garden maintenance? If so, you could consider becoming a house-sitter, looking after someone's home and pets while they are away on holiday – and getting paid for it. Put 'house sitter agency' into a search engine such as Google to find agencies specialising in this kind of work.

Internet teleworking Working with computers and the internet gives you a vast range of possibilities and potentially a worldwide customer base. You work in the comfort of your own home for customers in the next village or 12,000 miles away. You can write articles, write computer games, design brochures, edit a magazine, design website, create artwork, compose music, create accounts etc. And age is no barrier whatsoever. There are thousands of work opportunities out there on the net. Do a search on your particular expertise to see what is available.

But beware: there are hundreds of 'clubs' on the internet for every kind of freelance. Many of them will provide work for you, but many others will not. They will hook you with an offer of an initially free membership and then charge you a small regular monthly subscription rather than an annual fee. Once you have signed up it is easy to forget that you are making the payment, and after two or three months might be asking yourself if you are getting value for money.

Tread warily. Once you have sent the work, you cannot get it back. If your client is in another country you may have little or no protection if you do not get paid. So before doing any work, check things out properly. Establish good, mutually beneficial working relationships with your clients and you should be able to generate a comfortable income without leaving home.

Training for change It is becoming more and more common for people to acquire a new skill set in mid-life, or even post-retirement, in order to pursue a completely different career from they one they started out in. Ray, in his 50s and working for a voluntary organisation, trained in his spare time to qualify as a chiropodist. Maureen was a physicist. Now 72, she began to study bookkeeping after her retirement and is hoping to become self-employed on a part-time basis. She says restructuring her life after retirement has taken considerable time, budgeting and re-organisation.

Internet auction sales There are a number of auction sites, but the market leader by far is eBay. If you are a hoarder, or a collector, you could simplify your life by clearing out your loft and selling your unwanted possessions online. If you enjoy 'wheeling and dealing' and have basic computer skills you could easily supplement your income this way, or even start a brand-new business and earn a full-time income. Selling on eBay can generate a steady, though modest, income if you are prepared to put in the hours.

There are different ways of making an income using eBay:

■ **Sell new items** – if you have a special interest or expertise you might be able to find a manufacturer or a wholesaler who will supply you. You can set up an eBay shop and if your prices and service are right, people will beat a path to your door. For example, you might think about setting up an arrangement with a supplier of ceramic ornaments or crockery. Some people sell smoked salmon and prime beef: you might think of selling fresh haggis, or some other foodstuff not already on offer. One couple runs a business from home supplying a top brand of white goods, having set up a relationship with the manufacturer. They are able to undercut high street retailers and yet offer first-quality products with a full manufacturer's guarantee because the business is run from home in a converted garage and carries no stock: orders are just faxed over the manufacturer each day and the goods are delivered. This enterprise sells 15–20 dishwashers a day, together with fridges, freezers and cookers. Even if it were to clear only £10 per item, the earnings would be considerable.

- **Buy second-hand** on eBay, at car boot sales or at traditional auctions and re-sell them on eBay. Some people list items on eBay with poor descriptions and if you are prepared to do the searching you can pick up some bargains and re-sell them, but you must know what you are buying. If you know about antiques, you can pick up items from eBay and re-sell them, again on eBay, for a healthy profit. Bear in mind that if you do this sort of thing to generate a regular income, as opposed to now and again, HM Revenue and Customs will want you to register as self-employed and pay income tax. And do be sure that you know what you are buying and can re-sell the item: your objective is not to add to your own collections, but to make money.

- **Buy wholesale lots** of 'graded items' or catalogue returns on eBay and re-sell them through car boot sales or adverts in your local press. Most manufacturers are not interested in selling anything other than 'perfect' goods, and they also need to get rid of last year's models, which means there is a huge market in graded items, seconds or discontinued products. The manufacturers sell to distributors that have no interest in selling individual units, which is where you can come in. In the past, such items have been sold to market traders, but there is no reason why you cannot buy a job lot and re-sell on eBay at a profit, as long as you buy and sell smartly. Recent examples include a pallet of 35 top-brand vacuum cleaners for sale for £350 – just £10 each. Another pallet contained 75 hardware items with a RRP of £1,430 for sale for less than £200.

- **Work as an eBay trading assistant** Trading assistants sell things on eBay for other people and charge a commission. To become a trading assistant you need to have good experience of selling on eBay, a feedback score of at least 50 and at least 97 per cent positive feedback.

The downsides to selling on eBay are that it can take a lot more time than you would imagine to photograph items, write descriptions, upload the information and answer questions. The commissions and money-handling fees can cut big slices out of your profits, and it takes considerable time to pack and ship items. Packages can occasionally go missing in the post. None the less, you can sell to an international audience and you can achieve prices that you would never have thought possible. A company car advertised twice in the local newspaper produced not a single phone call, but once a good photograph and description had been posted on eBay it was sold for £500 more than the price asked in the newspaper, to someone who paid for it by bank transfer and arranged for a driver to collect it.

FLEXIBLE – NOT CASUAL – WORKING

For more about having a flexible working life, read *Jobshift* or *Creating You & Co.*, both by William Bridges.

Stepping out into the world as a self-employed person could be the most liberating and exhilarating experience of your life – or the biggest mistake you will ever make. Make sure you get it right by doing the groundwork and leaving nothing to chance. ∎

7

SOURCES OF FURTHER INFORMATION

CAREER AND LEGAL ADVICE

Help the Aged
Website: www.helptheaged.org.uk
The Charity campaigns on all aspects of age discrimination.

TAEN (The Age and Employment Network)
Tel: 020 7843 1590
Website: www.taen.org.uk
Supported by Help the Aged, TAEN is a leading centre of expertise on everything to do with age and employment, and a campaigning organisation, with a network of 250 member organisations, working for better opportunities for older people to continue working and learning.

ACAS (Advisory, Conciliation and Arbitration Service)
Helpline: 0845 7474747
Website: www.acas.org.uk
Publicly funded body that offers guidance on employment rights and legislation.

AdviceNow
Website: www.advicenow.org.uk
General advice, including legal issues such as age discrimination.

Age 2006
Website: www.age2006.org
Marking the year when the Employment Equality (Age) Regulations came into force, the site contains useful information for employees and employers.

Age Concern
Freephone helpline: 0800 009966
Scotland helpline: 0845 1259732
Website: www.ageconcern.org.uk

Age Positive
Website: www.agepositive.gov.uk
Government campaign promoting age diversity in employment, i.e. the benefits of employing a mixed-age workforce of both older and younger people. It encourages employers to make decisions about recruitment, training and retention that do not discriminate on basis of age. Website contains both legal advice and job-hunting tips (click on 'jobseeking').

Chartered Institute of Personnel and Development (CIPD)
Website: www.cipd.co.uk
Information on employment law and employees' rights.

Citizens Advice
Website: www.citizensadvice.org.uk
Three thousand bureaux throughout the UK.

Community Legal Advice
Tel: 0845 345 4345
Website: www.communitylegaladvice.org.uk
Provides legal information and advice on a range of issues. See also *Scottish Legal Aid Board* and *Northern Ireland Legal Services Commission*.

Directgov
Website: www.direct.gov.uk/en/Employment/Employees/ResolvingWorkplaceDisputes

/DG_10027992
Government website offering advice on grievance procedures.
Website:
www.direct.gov.uk/en/Over50s/index.htm
Information on pensions, job loss, looking for work, flexible working, learning and retirement planning.

Emplaw
Website: www.emplaw.co.uk
Free access to more than 4,500 cross-referenced 'fact cards' on British employment law, and facility for finding an employment lawyer in your area.

Employers' Forum on Age
Website: www.efa.org.uk
Information primarily aimed at employers, but also potentially helpful to others.

Equality and Human Rights Commission
This new body has taken over the work of the Commission for Racial Equality, the Disability Rights Commission and the Equal Opportunities Commission.
Website:
www.equalityhumanrights.org.uk

Law Centres Federation
Website: www.lawcentres.org.uk
Law Centres provide free independent legal advice and representation to disadvantaged people.

Law on the Web
Website: www.lawontheweb.co.uk
Legal advice.

The New Life Network
Website: www.newlifenetwork.co.uk
Advice on finding a new career direction.

Northern Ireland Legal Services Commission
Tel: 028 9040 8888
Website: www.nilsc.org.uk
Legal advice on a wide range of issues.

OneClickHR
Website: www.OneClickHR.com
Employment law and other issues, primarily for employers.

Samaritans
Tel. 08457 90 90 90 (UK); 1850 60 90 90 (Republic of Ireland)
Email: jo@samaritans.org
Website: www.samaritans.org.uk
Confidential, non-judgemental support, 24 hours a day, for people experiencing feelings of distress or despair.

Scottish Legal Aid Board
Tel: 0131 226 7061
Website: www.slab.org.uk
Legal information on a wide range of issues.

TAEN (The Age and Employment Network)
See page 210.

Trades Union Congress
Website: www.tuc.org.uk
Click on 'work rights' for information.

Tribunals Service

Website:
www.employmenttribunals.gov.uk
Government agency that provides all
the documentation and information
required to make a claim to an
employment tribunal, including form
ET1, which can be downloaded,
completed and submitted.

DISABILITY

The Ability Project – IT skills for
disabled people: www.ability.org.uk
Disability Now
www.disabilitynow.org.uk
Government www.disability.gov.uk
**National Bureau for Students
with Disabilities** www.skill.org.uk
**Royal Association for Disability
and Rehabilitation**
www.radar.org.uk

RECRUITMENT

There are many, but the following
are user-friendly, contain useful
information and feature many
thousands of UK job vacancies.

MAJOR RECRUITMENT SITES
Fish4jobs www.fish4jobs.co.uk
Jobcentre Plus (part of the
Department for Work and Pensions)
www.jobcentreplus.gov.uk
Jobsite www.jobsite.co.uk
Monster.co.uk www.monster.co.uk
Reed www.reed.co.uk
Totaljobs www.totaljobs.co.uk

OTHER 'AGE-POSITIVE' RECRUITMENT AGENCIES
40plus
Website: www.40plusrecruitment.co.uk
Agency with special focus on more
mature applicants, dealing with a range
of job roles from factory operative to
senior manager.

50plus People
Website: www.the50plus.co.uk
A 'route back into or a means of
staying in the workplace' for older
people, including a professional
property maintenance sub-site.

AgeThing
Website: www.agething.co.uk
This site, the name of which used to be
FiftyOn, features jobs, self-employment
opportunities, working at home,
working abroad and volunteering.

Careers Partnership (UK)
Website: www.careers-partnership-uk.com
Career management, human resources
outsourcing and psychometric
assessment services for individuals and
employers.

Centurenet
Website: www.centurenet.com
Recruitment service for older
employees looking for part-time or
full-time jobs, or opportunities to
work from home.

Executives Recycled
Website: www.executives-recycled.co.uk
Small site specialising in executives
and managers aged over 40 who are

looking for work or seeking a new challenge. Includes franchise opportunities.

The Job Portal
Website: www.the-job-portal.com
Links to the job vacancy pages of many UK employers.

Jobseeker Direct
Tel: 0845 6060234 (weekdays 8am–6pm, Sat 9am–1pm) (calls charged at local rates)
Website: wwwjobcentreplus.gov.uk
Part of the Department for Work and Pensions, this phone service keeps people in touch with the latest vacancies to help them find an appropriate job. It is particularly useful for those who are less comfortable about using the internet. Staff will explain how to apply, send you an application form and, where possible, ring the employer to arrange an interview.

Maturity Works
Website: www.maturityworks.co.uk
Small site for employers and jobseekers who believe that 'talent and ambition matter more than age'. See 'case studies' page for success stories of older career changers and employers with a positive view of age.

NHS Careers
Website: www.nhscareers.nhs.uk
Focuses on transferable skills and features stories of people who have started a second career in the NHS. The NHS is the UK's largest employer, with a requirement for skills in all disciplines and trades.

PosAbility
Website: www.posability.net
Commercial recruitment site for people with disabilities.

Prime50Plus
Website: www.prime50plus.co.uk
Matches the skills and experience of mature workers with the needs of employers.

PrimeXperience
Website: www.primexperience.co.uk
PrimeXperience is a part of Prime Recruitment Service, which also includes Prime50plus, Prime Professional (executive recruitment) and PrimeMploy (an online jobs board designed to minimise age, race and gender discrimination).

Principal People
Website: www.principalpeople.co.uk
Health, safety and environment recruitment agency.

Still Useful
Website: www.stilluseful.org
Links job seekers directly to the job vacancy pages of thousands of UK employers.

Wrinklies Direct
Website: www.wrinklies.org
Recruitment and employment agency for older people.

REGIONAL 'AGE-POSITIVE' RECRUITMENT AGENCIES
Agewise Recruitment
Website: www.agewiserecruitment.co.uk
Specialises in older job seekers (London).

Careers Springboard Aylesbury
Website:
www.careersspringboardaylesbury.
org.uk
Self-help group for redundant and
unemployed managers and
professionals in the Aylesbury area.

Dinosaurs Unlimited
Website: dinosaursunlimited.co.uk
Birmingham-based recruitment
agency for people over the age
of 45. Vacancies are primarily
midlands-based.

Equals One and Encore
Website:
www.equalsoneandencore.co.uk
Small online recruitment agency.
Most vacancies in Yorkshire area.

Kings Hill Recruitment
Website: www.khr.co.uk
Caters for the recruitment needs of
companies based on, and relocating
to, the Kings Hill Business Park, near
West Malling in Kent.

Know How Works
Website: www.know-howworks.co.uk
Jobs and advice plus links to many
local self-help groups, primarily in
the Thames Valley area.

Linda Taylor Associates
Website: www.lta-recruitment.co.uk
Full- and part-time vacancies
primarily in the North West of
England.

Wise Owls
Website: www.wiseowls.co.uk
Recruitment agency for over-45s that
also offers work placements/work
experience for those trying to get
back into work, links to training
courses (East and Central London)
and advice on business start-ups.

STARTING YOUR OWN BUSINESS

The British Franchise Association
Website: www.thebfa.org.
Information on franchising.

BT
Website:
http://sme.bt.com/startingabusiness
Useful resources for going it alone.

Business Angels Network
Website: www.VCR1978.com
Provides financing for business
start-ups.

Business Eye (Wales)
Tel. 0845 796 9798
Website: www.businesseye.org.uk
See Business Link for details.

Business Gateway (Scotland)
Tel: 0845 607 8787
Website: www.bgateway.com
See Business Link for details.

Business Link
Tel: 0845 600 9006
Website: www.businesslink.gov.uk
First port of call for anyone who
wants to start their own business.
It offers courses and advice on how to
start and grow a business along with
advice on grants available. It
is affiliated to other organisations

in Wales, Scotland and Northern Ireland: see *Business Eye, Business Gateway* and *Enterprise Northern Ireland.*

Business Planning Services
Website: www.bizplans.co.uk

Companies House
Website:
www.companieshouse.gov.uk
Contact to register a company.

Enterprise Northern Ireland
Tel: 028 7776 3555
Website: www.enterpriseni.com
See *Business Link* for details.

HM Revenue & Customs
Tel: 0845 915 4515
Website:
www.hmrc.gov.uk/startingup/index.htm
Runs a helpline for people who have become self-employed, where they can register and get help with tax, National Insurance and VAT. Other services include a nationwide network of business support teams and advice on tax credits. It is advisable to contact HM Revenue & Customs *before* going into business, in order to be clear about the obligations.

Patent Office
Website: www.patent.gov.uk
Contact to register a trademark or logo.

Prime
Tel: 0800 783 1904 (England and Scotland)
Website: www.primeinitiative.org.uk
Tel: 0845 601 8693 (Wales)
Website: www.prime-cymru.co.uk
Tel: 02890 267809 (Ireland)
Website: www.primebusinessclub.com
Helps people aged 50 and over to set up in business. Offers business support, advice on training and may be able to provide financial support as well.

UK Franchise Directory
Website:
www.theukfranchisedirectory.net

REHABILITATION OF OFFENDERS

NACRO
Website: www.nacro.org.uk
Previously the National Association for the Care and Resettlement of Offenders, Nacro works to tackle social exclusion and re-integrate offenders into society. Its website features a range of job opportunities.

See *also* legal websites in 'Career and legal advice' section above, and the **CIPD** factsheet for employers at http://crb.gov.uk/PDF/3083_Employing_aw.pdf

LIFESTYLE

Age-Net
Website: www.age-net.co.uk
Lifestyle site for over-50s.

NATIONAL NEWSPAPERS

Daily Express www.express.co.uk

Daily Mail www.dailymail.co.uk
Daily Mirror www.mirror.co.uk
Daily Telegraph
www.telegraph.co.uk
Financial Times www.ft.com
The Guardian
www.guardianunlimited.co.uk
Independent
www.independent.co.uk
Mail on Sunday
www.mailonsunday.co.uk
Sunday Mirror
www.sundaymirror.co.uk
Sunday Telegraph
www.sundaytelegraph.co.uk
Sunday Times www.sunday-
times.co.uk
The Observer www.observer.co.uk
The Times www.the-times.co.uk

PROFESSIONAL ONLINE JOURNALS AND NEWSPAPERS

Admin/secretarial:
www.londoncareers.net
Architectural: www.arplus.com
Automotive: www.motortrader.com
Entertainment and stage
performance: www.thestage.co.uk
Hospitality: www.caterer.com;
www.leisureweek.co.uk
Legal: www.lawgazette.co.uk;
www.the-lawyer.co.uk
Management consultancy:
www.managementconsultancy.co.uk
Marketing: www.marketingweek.co.uk
Media: www.nma.co.uk
Medicine: www.thelancet.com;
www.hsj.co.uk
Nursing: www.nursing-standard.co.uk
Personnel/HR:

www.peoplemanagement.co.uk;
www.personneltoday.com
Professional-level jobs:
www.economist.com
Public relations: www.prweek.com
Public finance: www.publicfinance.co.uk
Recruitment: www.professional-
recruiter.co.uk;
www.recruitermagazine.co.uk;
(online) www.onrec.com
Retail sales and marketing:
www.grocerjobs.co.uk
Scientific: www.naturejobs.com;
www.newscientistjobs.com;
http://sciencecareers.sciencemag.
org/career_development/
Supply management:
www.supplymanagement.co.uk
Teaching: www.tes.co.uk

LOCAL NEWSPAPERS

ENGLAND
Barnsley Chronicle www.barnsley-
chronicle.co.uk
Banbury Guardian
www.banburyguardian.co.uk
Barrow in Furness *Evening Mail*
www.nwemail.co.uk
Basildon Evening Echo
www.thisisessex.co.uk
Bath Chronicle www.thisisbath.com
Berwick Advertiser
www.tweeddalepress.co.uk
Bexhill Observer
www.bexhillobserver.co.uk
Birmingham Post and Mail
http://icbirmingham.icnetwork.co.uk/
Birmingham *The Metro*
www.metro.co.uk
Blackburn Citizen
www.thisislancashire.co.uk
Blackpool Citizen

www.thisislancashire.co.uk
Blackpool Gazette
www.blackpoolonline.co.uk
Bolton Evening News
www.thisislancashire.co.uk
Bradford (Yorks) Telegraph and Argus
www.thisisbradford.co.uk
Brighton Evening Argus
www.thisisbrighton.co.uk
Bristol Evening Post www.epost.co.uk
Bristol Western Daily Press
www.westpress.co.uk
Bromsgrove Advertiser
www.thisisworcestershire.co.uk
Buckingham Advertiser
www.buckinghamonline.co.uk
Buckinghamshire Bucks Free Press
www.thisisbuckinghamshire.co.uk
Buckinghamshire Bucks Herald
www.bucksherald.co.uk
Burnley Citizen
www.thisislancashire.co.uk
Bury St Edmunds Free Press
www.buryfreepress.co.uk
Bury Times www.burytimes.co.uk/jobs
Cambridge Evening News
www.cambridge-news.co.uk
Carlisle News and Star www.news-and-star.co.uk
Chester Chronicle
www.icchesteronline.co.uk
Chichester Observer
www.chiobserver.co.uk
Chorley Citizen
www.thisislancashire.co.uk
Colchester Evening Gazette
www.thisisessex.co.uk
Congleton Guardian
www.thisiswirral.co.uk
Cornwall Cornish Guardian
www.thisiscornwall.co.uk
Cornwall Cornish Weekly News
www.thisiscornwall.co.uk

Coventry Evening Telegraph
www.go2coventry.co.uk
Crewe Guardian
www.thisischeshire.co.uk
Cumberland and Westmorland Herald
www.cwherald.com
Cumberland News www.cumberland-news.co.uk
Darlington Northern Echo
www.thisisnortheastco.uk
Daventry Express
www.daventryonline.co.uk
Derby Evening Telegraph
www.chesterfieldtoday.co.uk
Derbyshire Times
www.chesterfieldtoday.co.uk
Devon (Mid) Gazette
www.middevongazette.co.uk
Devon (North) Journal
www.thisisnorthdevon.co.uk
Devon (South) Herald Express
www.thisissouthdevon.co.uk
Dewsbury Reporter
www.dewsburyreporter.co.uk
Dimbleby Newspapers
www.dimbleby.co.uk
Doncaster Free Press
www.doncasteronline.co.uk
Dorking Advertiser
www.dorkingadvertiser.co.uk
Droitwich Advertiser
www.thisisworcestershire.co.uk
Dudley News
www.thisistheblackcountry.co.uk
East Anglia Daily Times www.suffolk-now.co.uk
East Grinstead Observer
www.eastgrinsteadobserver.co.uk
Eastboume Herald
www.eastbourneherald.co.uk
Eastern Daily Press
http://new.edp24.co.uk
Eastwood and Kimberley Advertiser

www.eastwoodtoday.co.uk
Epsom and Banstead Herald
www.epsomherald.co.uk
Essex Chronicle www.thisisessex.co.uk
Evesham Advertiser
www.thisisworcestershire.co.uk
Exeter Express and Echo
www.thisisexeter:co.uk
Gateshead Post
http://icnewcastle.icnetwork.co.uk
Gloucester Citizen
www.thisisgloucestershire.co.uk
Gloucestershire Echo
www.thisisgloucestershire.co.uk
Grimsby Evening Telegraph
www.thisisgrimsby.co.uk
Guernsey Evening Press
www.guernsey-press.com
Halesowen News
www.thisistheblackcountry.co.uk
Hampshire Chronicle
www.thisishampshire.net
Harrogate Advertiser www.harrogate-advertiser-series.co.uk
Hemel Hempstead Gazette
www.hemelonline.co.uk
Hereford Times
www.thisishereford.co.uk
Horsham West Sussex County Times
www.horshamonline.co.uk
Hucknall and Bulwell Dispatch
www.hucknalltoday.co.uk
Huddersfield Daily Examiner
www.ichuddersfield.co.uk
Hull Daily Mail www.thisishull.co.uk
Ilkeston Advertiser
www.ilkestontoday.co.uk
Ilkley Gazette www.ilkleygazette.co.uk
Ipswich Evening Star
www.eveningstar.co.uk
Isle of Man News www.isle-of-man-newspapers.com
Isle of Wight County Press

www.thisishampshire.net
Jersey Evening Post
www.jerseyeveningpost.com
Keighley News www.keighleynews.co.uk
Kenilworth Weekly News
www.kenilworthonline.co.uk
Kent and East Sussex Courier
www.thisiskentandeastsussex.co.uk
Kidderminster The Shuttle
www.thisisworcestershire.co.uk
King's Lynn News www.lynnnews.co.uk
Knutsford Guardian
www.thisiswirral.co.uk
Lancashire (East) News
www.lancashireeveningtelegraph.co.uk
Lancashire Evening Post www.lep.co.uk
Lancashire Evening Telegraph
www.thisislancashire.co.uk
Lancaster Citizen
www.thisislancashire.co.uk
Lancaster Guardian
www.lancasteronline.co.uk
Leamington Spa Courier
www.leamingtononline.co.uk
Leatherhead Advertiser
www.leatherheadadvertiser.co.uk
Ledbury Advertiser
www.newsquestmidlands.co.uk
Leeds and Sheffield The Metro
www.metro.co.uk
Leicestershire Mercury
www.thisisleicestershire.co.uk
Leigh Journal www.thisislancashire.co.uk
Lincolnshire Echo
www.thisislincolnshire.co.uk
Liverpool Daily Post
http://icliverpool.icnetwork.co.uk
Liverpool Echo
http://icliverpool.icnetwork.co.uk
London – Guardian
www.guardianunlimited.co.uk
London – Newham Recorder
www.newhamrecorder.co.uk

London Newsquest Newspapers
www.thisislondon.co.uk
London (South) Press
www.southlondononline.co.uk
London *Evening Standard*
www.thisislondon.co.uk
London – *Hampstead & Highgate Express* www.hamhigh.co.uk
London *Weekend City Press Review*
www.news-review.co.uk
Ludlow Advertiser
www.newsquestmidlands.co.uk
Luton and Dunstable Herald
www.lutononline.co.uk
Maidenhead Advertiser
www.maidenhead-advertiser.co.uk
Malvern Gazette
www.thisisworcestershire.co.uk
Manchester Evening News
www.manchesteronline.co.uk
Mansfield Chronicle
www.mansfieldtoday.co.uk
Matlock Mercury
www.matlocktoday.co.uk
Mid-Sussex Times
www.midsussextimes.co.uk
Middlesbrough Evening Gazette
http://icteesside.icnetwork.co.uk
Midlands (West) *Express and Star*
www.westmidlands.com
Milton Keynes Citizen
www.mkcitizen.co.uk
Morecambe *Visitor News*
www.morecambeonline.co.uk
Newark Advertiser
www.newarkadvertiser.co.uk
Newbury Weekly News
www.newburynews.co.uk
Newcastle *Evening Chronicle*
www.evening-chronicle.co.uk
Newcastle upon Tyne Herald
www.herald-and-post.co.uk
Newcastle upon Tyne The Journal

www.thejournal.co.uk
Norfolk *Eastern Daily Press*
http://new.edp24.co.uk
North Cumberland Times www.times-and-star.co.uk
Northampton Chronicle & Echo
www.northamptonchronicleecho.co.uk
Northamptonshire Evening Telegraph
www.northamptonshireeveningteleg raph.co.uk
Northwich Guardian
www.norwichguardian.co.uk
Norwich Evening News
www.eveningnews24.co.uk
Nottingham Evening Post
www.thisisnottingham.co.uk
Ormskirk Maghull and Skelmersdale Advertiser
www.ormskirkadvertiser.co.uk
Oxford Mail www.thisisoxford.co.uk
Peterborough Evening Telegraph
www.peterboroughnet.co.uk
Plymouth Evening Herald
www.thisisplymouth.co.uk
Plymouth *Western Morning News*
www.westernmorningnews.co.uk
Portsmouth *The News*
www.thenews.co.uk
Preston Citizen
www.thisislancashire.co.uk
Reading Chronicle
www.readingchronicle.co.uk
Redditch Advertiser
www.thisisworcestershire.co.uk
Rugby Advertiser www.rugbyonline.com
Runcorn World www.thisiswirral.co.uk
Scunthorpe Evening Telegraph
www.thisisscunthorpe.co.uk
Sevenoaks Chronicle
www.thisiskentandeastsussex.co.uk
Sheffield Star www.sheffweb.co.uk
Shropshire Star

www.shropshirestar.co.uk
Skipton *Craven Herald*
www.cravenherald.co.uk
Slough and Langley Observer
www.thisisslough.com
Southampton *Southern Daily Echo*
www.dailyecho.co.uk
Southport Visiter
http://icseftonandwestlancs.
icnetwork.co.uk/visiter
St Albans and Harpenden Observer
www.stalbansobserver.co.uk
St Helens Star
www.thisislancashire.co.uk
Stafford Sentinel
www.thisisstafford.co.uk
Stourbridge News
www.thisistheblackcountry.co.uk
Stratford (Upon Avon) *Herald*
www.stratford-herald.co.uk
Stretford and Urmston Messenger
www.thisisstretford.co.uk
Sunderland Echo www.sunderland-echo.co.uk
Surrey Advertiser www.surreyad.co.uk
Surrey Mirror www.surreymirror.co.uk
Sussex Express
www.sussexexpress.co.uk
Swindon Business News www.swindon-business.net
Taunton Times www.thisistaunton.co.uk
Tenbury Advertiser
www.thisisworcestershire.co.uk
Tewkesbury Advertiser
www.thisisworcestershire.co.uk
Warwick Courier
www.warwickonline.co.uk
Watford Observer
www.watfordobserver.co.uk
Wellington Weekly News
www.thisisnorthdevon.co.uk
Westmorland Gazette
www.thisisthelakedistrict.co.uk

Wharfedale Observer
www.wharfedaleobserver.co.uk
Whitehaven News www.whitehaven-news.co.uk
Widnes World www.thisiswirral.co.uk
Wigan Observer www.wigantoday.net
Wiltshire Evening Advertiser
www.thisiswiltshire.co.uk
Wiltshire Gazette and Herald
www.thisiswiltshire.co.uk
Wiltshire Times
www.thisiswiltshire.co.uk
Winsford Guardian
www.winsfordguardian.co.uk
Wirral Globe www.thisiswirral.co.uk
Worcester Evening News
www.thisisworcester.co.uk
Worcester News
www.thisisworcestershire.co.uk
Worksop Guardian
www.worksopguardian.co.uk
Worthing Herald
www.worthingherald.co.uk
Yeovil Clarion www.yeovil-clarion-today.co.uk
Yeovil Western Gazette
www.westgaz.co.uk
York Evening Press www.thisisyork.co.uk
Yorkshire Evening Post www.yorkshire-evening-postco.uk
Yorkshire Post www.ypn.co.uk

NORTHERN IRELAND
Belfast Telegraph
www.belfasttelegraph.co.uk
Fermanagh Herald
www.fermanaghherald.com
Fermanagh Impartial Reporter
www.impartialreporter.com
Irish News www.irishnews.com
Northern Ireland Alpha Group
www.ulsternet-ni.co.uk
Ulster Herald www.ulsterherald.com

SCOTLAND
Aberdeen and District Independent www.mediauk.com/newspapers/41510/aberdeen-and-district-independent
Aberdeen Press and Journal www.thisisnorthscotland.co.uk
Borders Southern Reporter www.tweeddalepress.co.uk
Dundee Courier www.thecourier.co.uk
Dunoon Evening Telegraph www.eveningtelegraph.co.uk
Dunoon Observer www.dunoon-observer.co.uk
Falkirk Herald www.falkirkherald.co.uk
Fife Free Press www.fifefreepress.co.uk
Glasgow Evening Times www.eveningtimes.co.uk
Hawick News www.hawick-news.co.uk
Shetland Times www.shetlandtoday.co.uk
Stornoway Gazette www.stornowaygazette.co.uk

Scotland national newspapers
Daily Record www.record-mail.co.uk
Sunday Herald www.sundayherald.com
Sunday Mail www.record-mail.co.uk
Sunday Post www.sundaypost.com
The Herald www.theherald.co.uk
The Scotsman www.scotsman.com
Scotland on Sunday www.scotlandonsunday.com
Scottish and Universal Newspapers www.inside-scotland.co.uk

WALES
Denbighshire Free Press www.denbighshirefreepress.co.uk
Bangor Chronicle www.northwaleschronicle.co.uk
Flintshire Standard www.flintshirestandard.co.uk
Llanelli Star www.tindlenews.co.uk
Oswestry and Border Advertiser www.bordercountiesadvertiser.co.uk
Powys County Times www.countytimes.co.uk
Rhyl Journal www.rhyljournal.co.uk
North Wales Chronicle www.northwaleschronicle.co.uk
North Wales Pioneer www.northwalespioneer.co.uk
Wales (South) *Evening News* www.thisissouthwales.co.uk
Wales (South) *Pioneer* www.thisissouthwales.co.uk
Wrexham Evening Leader www.eveningleader.co.uk

Wales national newspapers
Western Mail and Echo www.totalwales.com

TRAINING PROVIDERS/ LEARNING AND SKILLS DEVELOPMENT ADVICE

Academy of Learning
Website: www.academyoflearning.co.uk
Search on 'training programmes': some, such as those for qualifications with the Institute of Leadership and Management, are free or fully funded.

BBC Education Learning Zone
Website: www.bbc.co.uk/education/lzone
BBC2's unique overnight-record and play service enables users to learn at their leisure.

BTEC/Edexcel

Website: www.edexcel.org.uk
For vocational qualifications. Contains details of courses and training course providers.

City and Guilds

Website: www.city-and-guilds.co.uk
Providers of vocational training courses. Search website for suitable qualifications, then enter postcode to find addresses of local providers.

Department for Children, Schools and Families

Website: www.dfes.gov.uk
Disregarding the name, click on the link for higher education students for information about college/university courses.

Experience Matters

Website:
www.experiencematters.org.uk
A training consultancy that focuses on the over-50s.

learndirect

Websites: www.learndirect.co.uk;
www.learndirect-advice.co.uk
For information and advice on upgrading skills, careers or starting a business. Signposts thousands of courses.

Lifelong Learning

Website: www.lifelonglearning.co.uk
Click on 'older learners' for useful links.

New Deal

Tel: 0845 606 2626 (7am–11pm) for information pack (or see website)

Website:
www.jobcentreplus.gov.uk/JCP/Customers/New_Deal/
Government initiatives for people who have been unemployed for six months or more.

NIACE (National Institute of Adult and Continuing Education)

Tel: (England) 0116 204 4200;
(Wales) 0292 0370900
Website: www.niace.org.uk
A non-governmental organisation that promotes adult learning in England and Wales. Provides information on the new legislation in relation to education and training, and links to numerous learning and development organisations.

Open University

Website: www3.open.ac.uk/courses
No matter what your previous background, you can take foundation courses to enable you to study for degree-level qualifications and beyond.

Over50.gov.uk

Website: www.over50.gov.uk
Government website designed to help people get the most out of their working lives and leisure time, with information on and contact details for community and voluntary organisations, as well as training opportunities and health and fitness advice.

ThirdAge

Website: www.thirdage.com
Workshops and courses on a range of subjects.

Third Age Challenge
Website: www.thirdagers.net
Not-for-profit organisation that supports people who are unemployed or likely to become so. Free training workshops in Swindon.

Third Age Foundation
Website: www.thirdage.org.uk
For skills development (especially computer skills). Information and links to many useful courses (London).

University of Strathclyde Centre for Life Long Learning
Website: www.cll.strath.ac.uk/ssi.html
Offers an extensive range of educational opportunities for older adults.

University of the Third Age
Website: www.u3A.org.uk
A self-help organisation for people no longer in full-time employment, U3A provides educational, creative and leisure opportunities.

Wrinklies
Website: http://wrinklies.co.uk
An online community and learning resource open to anyone. Main objective is to help people use computers and the internet more effectively.

RESEARCHING COMPANIES

Kompass
Website: www.compass.com
Site features 2.2 million companies in 70 countries referenced by 54,000 product and service keywords, 822,000 trade names and 4.2 million executive names.

SELF-ANALYSIS FOR CAREER AND LIFE PLANNING

Keirsey Temperament Sorter
Website: www.keirsey.com
Access the Keirsey Temperament Sorter (personality evaluation) at this site.

Portfolio working
Website: www.creativekeys.net/portfoliocareertest.htm
Take the self-test to see whether portfolio working would suit you.

Eos Career Services
Website: www.eoslifework.co.uk/getalife.xls
Analyse your work/life balance and design your ideal life pie by following this link to a Microsoft Excel tool.

SKILLS AND APTITUDE TESTS

The following organisations are respected producers of instruments used by some organisations in the selection process:

ASE

Website: www.ase-
solutions.co.uk/support.asp
Choose 'Practice tests'.

SHL

Website: www.shl.com
Click on the tab 'Practice tests'.

AGE-POSITIVE EMPLOYERS

Website:
www.agepositive.gov.uk/champions/in
dex.asp
Age Positive Employer Champions
are employers and organisations that
have demonstrated their
commitment to tackling age
discrimination and promoting age
diversity in the workplace.

NETWORKING WEBSITES/CLUBS

Chambers of Commerce

Website: www.chamberonline.co.uk
Contact your local chamber of
commerce for networking
opportunities and details of any
networking clubs in your area.

Friends Reunited

Website: www.friendsreunited.co.uk
Track down old friends. This
organisation now claims 19 million
members. Linked to it is a business
networking site with 12 million
members (www.linkedin.com).

VOLUNTARY WORK

The following are just a few
possibilities. For many thousands
more volunteering opportunities, put
'voluntary work' into an internet
search engine.

Do-it

Website: www.do-it.org.uk
UK volunteering possibilities.

Gap Year for Grown-ups

Website:
www.GapYearForGrownUps.co.uk
Career break opportunities and
volunteer projects worldwide.

I Want to Volunteer

Website: www.idealist.org
International opportunities.

Médecins Sans Frontières

Website:
www.msf.org/unitedkingdom

VSO (Voluntary Service Overseas)

Website: www.vso.org.uk

Worldwide Volunteering

Website: www.wwv.org.uk

Note The internet changes all the
time: as one website closes down,
another ten open to take its place.
Some of these links may therefore
become inactive. If you let us know
we can amend the text for the
next edition of this guide (email
the author at Malcolm@Delta-
Management.co.uk). Similarly,
suggestions for inclusions in this

listing would be welcome via the same email address.

Inclusion of an organisation/website in this directory does not constitute an endorsement by the author or the publisher.

All the websites listed in this chapter can be linked to via the website www.hornby.org (click on Working at 50+).

PUBLICATIONS
Body language
Allan and Barbara Pease have written a number of good books on body language, including *The Definitive Book of Body Language* (2005).
Leadership
The Situational Leader (1992) by Dr Paul Hersey
Leadership and the One-minute Manager (2000) by Kenneth Blanchard, Patricia Zigarmi, and Drea Zigarmi
Both titles advocate a flexible leadership approach.

Self-employment
Lloyds TSB Small Business Guide (regularly updated) by Sara Williams
The Complete Small Business Guide: a sourcebook for new and small businesses: (2005) by Colin Barrow
From Acorns: how to build your brilliant business from scratch (2003) by Caspian Woods
Start Your Business: week by week (2004) by Steve Parks
White Ladder Diaries: the pain and pleasure of launching a business (2005) by Ros Jay and (editor) Richard Craze

Anyone Can Do It: building Coffee Republic from our kitchen table: 57 real-life laws on entrepreneurship (2002) by Sahar and Bobby Hashemi
Jobshift: how to prosper in a workplace without jobs (1994) or *Creating You & Co.: be the boss of your own career* (1997), both by William Bridges.

Age discrimination
How to Recognise Cases of Age Discrimination, in which Help the Aged and TAEN were involved, is available at www.taen.org.uk/publications/ad_guide_for_workers.pdf

APPENDICES

APPENDIX I
EMPLOYMENT TIPS FROM A
SPECIALIST RECRUITMENT AGENCY

The Government estimates that two-thirds of the growth in the UK workforce in the years to 2017 will have to come from older workers and/or immigrant labour.

Currently one million older people of working age are unemployed in the UK.

The agency Working Links, which specialises in getting older people back into work, has found in working with job seekers of 50+ that, in common with all groups of people who experience difficulty accessing employment, ideal working patterns and the barriers to work are different for each individual.

In workshops conducted by this agency with job seekers aged over 50, several common themes emerged:

- lack or loss of confidence
- long period of unemployment
- pride and perception of available opportunities
- lack of training and outdated skills
- lack of motivation.

The following questions were put by the author to the agency's Director for Partnerships, Sandra Moore:

1 What can older applicants do to increase their chances of selection?
This will always depend on the individual and their personal circumstances. However, our experience leads us to believe that a tailored mix including some of the following activities will improve an applicant's chance of selection.

Participation in self-help groups These can be made up of people experiencing a wide range of difficulties in accessing employment. Together, they can begin to tackle issues such as lack of motivation and loss of confidence.

Review how they personally view age Consider yourself as being at a stage in your life (as opposed to an age) and promote your age as positive by highlighting transferable skills and experience.

Research the potential employer Gain an understanding of the application and interview process. Ask for advice on and rehearse any unfamiliar recruitment and selection techniques: for example, telephone and internet sifts and competency-based interviews. Adopt a flexible approach, remembering that things may have changed since your last interview.

CVs and application forms CVs and application forms that are tailored to reflect the job and person specification have a much better chance of resulting in an interview.

Language Everyone who is trying to make a good impression should promote themselves in the best way. Avoid phrases such as 'I know I'm old but . . .' and 'Just because I'm over 50 . . .'.

Consider a work trial Ask for an opportunity to show, rather than telling the employer at the interview, what you can do. Once in the working environment you have a unique opportunity to demonstrate the added value you can bring. There is a lot to said for a 'get in and get on' attitude.

Undertake a skills check Consider re-training and developing IT skills if these are needed to compete for the job.

2 Have you any examples of older candidates 'de-selecting' themselves because of things they have done, written or said in the selection process?

Often the de-selection process happens when the applicant is looking at the range of opportunities available. Candidates will often de-select themselves on the basis that they do not believe that they should even apply at their age.

Feedback from interviews generally does not highlight issues relating solely to the age of the applicant. There is, however, a perception that older workers do not always promote themselves at interview, believing that their experience should 'speak for itself'.

One employer did say that a candidate who was over the age of 50 did not speak enough at the interview. The candidate later said that he did not think he needed to say much as the employer had his CV and knew what he could do.

3 Have you any examples of older employees reducing their employability because of Luddite* attitudes or similar?

In common with people of all ages older employees do not always recognise the need to re-train or develop new skills in order to maintain their effectiveness in the ever-changing working environment. Additionally, unemployed older workers have told us that personal pride means that they are unwilling to undertake what they consider to be menial tasks; they have been resistant to retraining, preferring to continue to try to remain in their existing job role. They also have misconceptions about job roles – for example, believing that call centre work is a younger person's job and that they would not fit in.

4 Have you any examples of best practice in the context of employing older people?

Employers naturally want to attract people with the appropriate skills and experience. Modern recruitment practice in conjunction with new legislation is designed to ensure that age is not a deciding factor in the selection process. Increasingly, companies are recognising that age diversity provides a wide vari-

*Luddite: one who opposes technical or technological change. After Ned Ludd, an English labourer who in 1779 destroyed weaving machinery in the belief that technological advance would bring unemployment.

ety of skills and experience and provides them with a competitive edge. By balancing age and experience within teams employers benefit from the older worker's ability to make decisions based on experience, to problem-solve and to mentor and coach colleagues. This promotes a stable and happy workforce and increased levels of retention of valuable employees. Interestingly, while older workers can sometimes feel that their age is a barrier to employment, training and/or promotion younger people also believe this to be true for them.

Best practice for recruitment and employment includes:

- flexible working patterns for existing and new members of staff
- removal of personal details (address, age, etc.) from paperwork presented to selection and interview panels
- publication of vacancies in ways that will reach people of a variety of ages
- monitoring of the age of the workforce
- use of selection criteria to record answers to interview questions
- ensuring that training and development are equally available to all members of staff.
- planning for retirement in a constructive and open partnership.

APPENDIX II
SAMPLE LEARNING LOG

John Brown, portfolio worker (self-employed): HR consultant, writer, foster carer, internet auctioneer and property developer.

'*When we stop learning we stop living*.' This log features key learning experiences. It does not include regular email updates from the HR internet forums to which John Brown belongs or his regular reading of journals from professional institutes.

Month	Event/process	Organiser/ speaker	Learning outcome(s): what I will do as a result
January	Career and Life Planning seminar	CIPD	1 Reappraise work/life balance and own financial needs and goals
February	Employment Law Update	CIPD	1 Re-write article on discipline/ termination 2 Further research on ACAS website re new employment tribunal
March	Speed Networking Negotiating	CIPD HQ	1 SN not for me – discuss with CIPD colleagues 2 Review and rewrite negotiation skills materials for my seminars
	Grow Your Business conference	Business Link – Steve Parks & Roger Black	1 Rewrite own business goals
April	Pension Update	CIPD	1 Significant re-appraisal of personal pension and retirement plans 2 Advise clients in terms of long-term employment/pension-planning strategies

Month	Event/process	Organiser/ speaker	Learning outcome(s):
May	eBay University for Powersellers – one-day conference	eBay	1 Target high-value/low-volume products to sell – esp. antique silver 2 Differentiate products through use of advertising features 3 Use turbo-lister
June	Fostering Training correspondence course	Social Care	1 Personal implications of fostering – recognise impact on own relationships 2 Legal implications of fostering – keep meticulous records
July	Communication Skills conference	CIPD	1 Methods of structuring a presentation/ lecture – use of video clips for training sessions 2 Read/research NLP further to challenge my own paradigms about its role/usefulness
August	Attachment Disorder workshop	Social Care	1 Recognise symptoms 2 Beware of needs of child; create and leave space for child to grow
September			
October	Buy-to-Let seminar	Belvoir Property Management	1 Identify correct property and target young professionals market – develop and sell current property 2 Expand portfolio in light of new pension legislation

Note John Brown's philosophy is that if he does one thing differently and better after attending a learning event, that event has been of value to him.

APPENDIX III
AGE DISCRIMINATION LEGISLATION

The Employment Equality (Age) Regulations 2006 came into force on 1 October 2006. The legislation was deemed necessary to counteract ageist behaviour and practices, either conscious or unintentional, in the workplace. The regulations apply to all employers, private and public sector, vocational training providers, trade unions, professional and employer organisations and managers of occupational pension schemes.

There is now a national default retirement age of 65, which should not be confused with 'pension age'. This renders it unlawful for an employer to insist upon compulsory retirement below that age. Protection is provided for those applying for employment and for those already employed. An employee has the right to request to work beyond 65 or any other retirement age set by the company. In turn, the employer has to consider this request under a 'duty to consider procedure'.

There are two types of age discrimination, namely:

- direct: treating someone less favourably because of their age
- indirect: having a policy or practice that puts people of a certain age group at a disadvantage, compared to other people.

There are a very few circumstances when it is lawful to treat people differently because of age, the main ones being:

- objective justification — the employer may have fixed a maximum age for the recruitment or promotion of employees to reflect the training requirements of the post or the need for a reasonable period of employment before retirement;
- genuine occupational requirement: for example, an actor playing the part of a person of a particular age;
- where there is a need for 'positive action' by the employer i.e. targeting recruitment at older people as long as the position itself is open to all ages;
- if a job applicant is within six months of the employer's normal retirement age (if the employer has one) or the age of 65, an employer may refuse to recruit on the grounds of age;

Q *What should I do if I feel that I am being discriminated against in the recruitment process?*
A The DTI's website is a good starting point. It contains a questionnaire which can be completed and returned to the employer for their response. You may

need help completing this form from a solicitor or other employment specialist. You should in any event seek assistance upon receipt of the response from the employer to consider an application to the employment tribunal, which has to be made within three months of the discriminatory act.

Q *What should I do if I feel that I am being discriminated against in my workplace?*
A You should speak to the person concerned informally. If the problem persists, speak to your manager. You may then wish to make a formal complaint using the grievance procedure. If the grievance procedure has been exhausted, you may want to consider making a claim to the employment tribunal. If you do, be sure to bear in mind the time limits.

EMPLOYERS

All employers are now required by law to make sure they have fair procedures in place to avoid discrimination on grounds of age. Some of the positive steps being taken by employers to comply with the new legislation might include:

■ revising recruitment, selection and promotion criteria: for example, removing dates of birth, periods of employment and other indicators of age from application forms to ensure that shortlisting decisions are based on skills and abilities alone;
■ updating the following policies to include age discrimination:
   equality
   harassment, bullying and victimisation
   training
   removing upper age limits from unfair dismissal
      and redundancy payments
   pay, benefits and other employment conditions
   the 'duty to consider' procedure (for managers).

As the age discrimination regulations are relatively new, it is too early to assess their effectiveness, but the introduction of legislation is a positive step and shows the Government is taking this area of employment law very seriously.

Denise Brosnan, Partner, Buller Jeffries Solicitors

INDEX

– a message for age-positive organisations

Engage is a unique and revolutionary business network set up by Help the Aged in response to the changing demographic of our society. It offers expertise to businesses that deal with the 50+ generation.

Engage works with forward-thinking organisations to meet the needs – and the opportunities represented by – the changing marketplace.

It offers:
- ❏ information-sharing
- ❏ access to expertise
- ❏ free seminars on different aspects of best practice
- ❏ help with writing in-house training manuals
- ❏ support at design stage for products and services, to ensure that they are age-aware.

Engage also offers accreditation and kite-marking for age-positive businesses. Its members include many of the world's largest and highest-profile companies, but it welcomes organisations of any size.

For further information, visit our site at
http://corporate.helptheaged.org.uk/engage
or contact: Engage at Help the Aged,
207–221 Pentonville Road, London N1 9UZ